PREFACE

The Rag-Ragini System came into existence in 12th century A.D. and even now this is the main system being followed. According to this system there are six main Ragas. Each Raga has five Raginis associated with it. They are supposed to be their wives. There are other minor Ragas associated with each Ragini as its sons' wives, this is a kind of family structure in the world of Indian Music.

In the beginning of 20th century A.D. several music conferences were held to modify the Rag-Ragini system. Ragas were categorised according to the number of notes used in those Ragas. The new system is known as Thata system and is now popular in whole of India. In fact Thata system is the basis of present day north Indian music. The names of ragas in Thata system are the same as in older Rag-Ragini system.

According to Viyankat Mukhee in South Indian music there are seventy two different Thatas. But north Indian musicians don't accept two forms of the same note in one Thata and therefore according to them there are only thirty two separate Thatas. Out of these thirty two Thatas only ten are prominent and all important and popular ragas belong to these ten Thatas. The north Indian system was propagated by V.N. Bhatkhande.

The present work is based on Kramik Pustika of V.N. Bhatkhande (in 6 volumes) which is recognised as standard work by all music institutions of India. All essential details of 200 Ragas have been clearly and concisely given for the benefit of beginners as well as the advanced students of music. The book is self-sufficient and contains hints regarding all aspects of ragas. We hope that the book will certainly prove a welcome addition to music literature.

RAM AVTAR 'VIR'
Sangeetacharya

COMPARATIVE TECHNICAL MUSIC WORDS USED IN THIS BOOK

Sl. No.	Indian Words		Comparative English Words
	Hindi	Roman	
1.	नाद	Nada	Musical Sound
2.	श्रुति	Shruti	Microtonic Interval
3.	स्वर	Swara	Note
4.	शुद्धस्वर	Shudh Swara	Full tone note
5.	कोमलस्वर	Komal Swara	Half tone note
6.	तीव्रस्वर	Tivra Swara	Sharp note
7.	सप्तक	Saptaka	Octave
8.	अतिमंद्रसप्तक	Atimandra Saptaka	Double Lower Octave
9.	मन्द्रसप्तक	Mandra Saptaka	Lower Octave (Bass clef)
10.	मध्यसप्तक	Madhya Saptaka	Medium Octave
11.	तारसप्तक	Tar Saptaka	Upper Octave
12.	ठाठ	Thata	Scale
13.	राग	Raga	Tune
14.	रागअलाप	Raga Alap	Improvisation of Raga
15.	आरोह	Aroh	Ascent
16.	अवरोह	Avaroh	Descent
17.	पकड़	Pakad	Dominating notes of Ragas
18.	स्थाई	Sthai	First Part of a song or tune
19.	अन्तरा	Antra	Second part of a song or tune
20.	लय	Laya	Rhythm
21.	विलम्बितलय	Vilambit Laya	Slow Rhythm
22.	मध्य लय	Madhya Laya	Medium Rhythm
23.	द्रुतलय	Drut Laya	Fast Rhythm
24.	ताल	Tala	Time
25.	ताली	Tali	Clapping of hands
26.	खाली	Khali	Silent Beat
27.	मात्रा	Matra	Beat (one second time)
28.	खण्ड	Khand	Bar
29.	सम	Sam	Starting point of a tala
30.	कम्पन	Kampan	Vibration
31.	मींड	Meend	Meend
32.	वादीस्वर	Vadi Swara	King note
33.	सम्वादीस्वर	Samvadi Swara	Harmonic Note
34.	विवादीस्वर	Vivadi Swara	Dissonant Note
35.	वर्जितस्वर	Varjit Swara	Omitted Note.

CONTENTS

ALPHABETICAL CONTENTS

1

Bilawal Thata

Sa Re Ga Ma Pa Dha Nee Sa

Bilawal Raga is also called Shankara Bharan (Mel Raga). At the time of Raga-Ragini system in Hanuman Mata Bilawal was considered as Ragini of Hindole Raga. Now-a-days Bilawal is a Thata Vachak Raga and includes 35 Ragas out of which 8 are more popular.

Shudh Bilawal—Alhiya Bilawal—Behag—Shankara—Deshkar—Hem—Yaman Bilawal Devgiri—Odavdevgiri—Sarparda—Lachhasakh—Shukal Bilawal — Kaukab — Nut Bilawal — Nut Behag—Nut Kamode—Nut Kedar—NUT—Nut Narain—Behagda—Pat Behag—Maloha Jaldhar—Durga—Gunkali—Pahadi—Mand—Savani—Mulla—Chhaya—Chhaya Tilak—Mewada—Patmanjiri—Hansdhwani—Deepak.

1. *Shudh Bilawal*
2. *Alhiya Bilawal*
3. *Behag*
4. *Shankara*
5. *Deshkar*
6. *Pahadi*
7. *Durga*
8. *Mand*

It is the Raga of *Shant* or peaceful nature dominating in Bhakti Rasa. It is very useful for beginners. It is a morning melody and stress is laid upon the uttarang. The beauty of the uttarang Ragas lies chiefly in its Avaroh—Sa Nee Dha Pa. It is best to start with the Bilawal Scale, the Vibration of each tone is more or less uniform and to acquire the full tones mentally and musicaly is the first step of importance.

1. *Shudh Bilawal* is the That Rag and owes its origin in Bilawal, the port in Kathiawar. It is more or less obscure. It is called the morning Kalyan. It is a beautiful melody and lends itself to difficult styles and Tanas (variations), suited to male and female voices. In Kalyan, ga is strong, in Bilawal, dha is strong and nee is wakra (crooked) in Aroh. It is uttarang, hence the chief beauty lies in Avaroh.

Jati—Sampoorna *Vadi*—Dha, *Samvadi*—Ga, *Time*—Morning

Aroh—S, R, G, M, P, D, N, S̩.

Avaroh—SND, PMG, RS.

Pakad—GR, GP, D, NS.

2. *Alhiya Bilawal* is a popular extremely attractive melody, usually kown and sung as Bilawal, Ma, is dropped in Aroh, and Nee (komal), is inserted in the Avaroh, and it becomes Alhiya. This delicate distinction between the two Ragas, is known to the experts. It is rendered in difficult styles and suited to both voices.

Jati—Sampoorna, *Vadi*—Dha, *Samvadi*—Ga, *Time*—Morning.

Aroh—S, R, G, R, GP, NP, NS,

Avaroh—SND, P, DNDP, MG, MR, S.

Pakad—GR, GP, D, NS.

3. *Behag* is an extremely pretty melody lends itself to all styles, and Alap (variations), in the 3 Octaves, suitable for female voices, Re, and Dha, are dropped in the Aroh, Ga, plays an important part, Nee, forms the basis of Tanas Ma, (Tivra) is occasionally used lending additional charm. Both Ma are used with charming effect.

Jati—Odava Sampoorna, *Vadi*—Ga, *Samvadi*—Nee *Time*—Night.

Aroh—SG, MP, NS.

Avaroh—S, NDP, MG, RS.

Pakad—NS, GMP, GMG, RS.

4. *Shankara* is a serious melody and lends itself to difficult styles, more fit for male voices. It is a dignified impressive Raga, and sounds well in Bilampat (Rhythm). There are two kinds of Shankara, one is Odava, which drops Re, and Ma, and the other one drops Ma. Shankara, is something like Malsari and Behag, and yet quite distinct.

Jati—Shadava Sampooran, *Vadi*—Ga, *Samvadi*—Nee, *Time*—Night

Aroh—SG, P, ND, S.

Avaroh—S NP, ND, S, NP, GP, GS.

Pakad—S, NP, ND, S, NP, GP, GS.

5. *Deskar* is different to Des, and must not be confused. It lends itself well to Gazal and Thumri, style of singing fit for female voices. It is a pretty melody, drops Ma, and Nee in the scale, and is the counterpart of Bhoopali which also drops Ma, and Nee. The distinguishing feature of both melodies lies in giving prominence to the Vadi Swara (king note). Deskar, takes, Dha, as vadi and is a morning tune. Bhoopali, takes, Ga, and is an evening tune. The Dha, Pa combination is a pleasing characteristic.

Jati—Odava, *Vadi*—Dha, *Samvadi* Ga, *Time*—Day.

Aroh—SRG, P, DS.

Avaroh—SD, P, GPDP, GRS.

Pakad—D, P, GP, GRS.

6. *Hem* is called Hem Kalyan also. It is obscure. Vadi is Sa, and Dha, Nee are dropped in Aroh and Nee and Ga, are dropped in Avaroh. There is a resemblance of Kalyan and Kamode, in 'Hem'.

Jati : Odava—*Vadi*—Sa, *Samvadi*—Pa, *Time*—Night

Aroh PDP, SRS, GMP, DPS.

Avaroh SDP, GMP, G M R S.

Pakad : SDP, DM, MRS.

7. *Yaman Bilawal* is obscure and takes both Ma. Its vadi is Sa. It is a mixture of Yaman and Bilawal. In Aroh it is Yaman and Avaroh it is like Bilawal and this makes its special feature. An obscure melody should only be rendered by experts.

Jati:—Wakra Sampoorna. *Vadi*—Sa, *Samvadi*—Pa, *Time*—Morning.

Aroh—S, RG, MG, MPD, NDS.

Avaroh—NDP, MG, MRS.

Pakad—NDP, MG, MRS.

8. *Dev Giri* is known only to the experts and hardly ever heard and therefore, not popular. It is an obscure variety of Bilawal, and possesses a tune of Kalyan, and is therefore something like Yaman Bilawal. All these delicate differences tend to point to the main feature of the Raga and therefore, should be noted carefully. Vadi is Sa, the secret of singing these classical Ragas, is known to experts.

Jati—Odava Sampoorn, *Vadi*—Sa, *Samvadi*—Pa, *Time*—Day.

Aroh—SNDND, MRG, GMG, PDNDS.

Avaroh—SNDNP, MGMRS.

Pakad—SD, SRGMRS.

9. *Odava Dev Giri*—Odava Dev Giri is the other type of Dev Giri in which Dha and Ga are prohibited.

10. *Sarparda* is a favourite melody with the Sitar players as the style of Gut Todas can be rendered well and this style is exclusive for 'Sitar'. It is a pretty fascinating tune. Sar in Persian is Chief and Parda is the bar indicating the different notes on Sitar. Sarparda is the chief bar. It is a mixture of Yaman Bilawal and Goud, and is an invention of Amir Khusro.

Jati—Sampoorna *Vadi*—Sa, *Samvadi*—Pa, *Time*—Morning.

Aroh—S R G M, D P D N S.

Avaroh—S N D P, N D P, D P M, GMRS

Pakad—S R GM, D D P M, PM, GGRS.

11. *Lachha Sakh* is not so very popular, but lends it self to easy styles. There are one or two famous Tirwat and Sargams constituted in this melody supposed to be very ancient. It is a mixture of Jhinjoti and Bilawal. Both Nee, are used, Dha is vadi. Like Sarparda, the Bilawal tune must be clearly shown in Lachchha Sakh also. It is invention of Amir Khusro.

Jati Sampoorna—*Vadi*—Dha, *Samvadi*—Ga, *Time*—Morning.

Aroh—S R G M P, M P M G, D N D N S.

Avaroh—SNDDP, DDPMGRS.

Pakad : SRGMP, GMPGR, GRS.

12. *Shukal Bilawal* is only known to the experts, like Dev Giri, Nut and Nut Bilawal and therefore not at all popular, is obscure; Ma is Vadi, Re is weak in Aroh, it is Uttarang Raga therefore its chief beauty lies in its Avaroh, the Dha, Ma, glide is its speciality. Its formation is wakra (crooked) therefore resembles Goud Sarang, and a slight tinge of Nee, lends an additional charm.

Jati—Wakra Shadava Sampoorna, *Va li*—Ma, *Samvadi*—Sa, *Time*—Morning.

Aroh SGM, MPNDP, DNS.

Avaroh—SNDNDP, MGR, MRS.

Pakad—SGMMRP, DNDP, MGR, MRS.

13. *Kaukab* is known only to a few experts, therefore obscure. This is also a variety of Bilawal. Its Vadi is Ma and Samvadi is Sa, and the combination of Re, and Pa, must be shown occasionally, Re, Ga, and Ma, are tremulous, Ga, is dropped in Aroh. It is an invention of Amir Khusro.

Jati—Shadava Sampoorna, *Vadi*—Ma, *Samvadi*—Sa, *Time*—Morning.

Aroh—SRRP, MPDNDS.

Avaroh—SNDP, MPMGMGMRS.

Pakad—SRR, DP, MPDP, GRRS.

14. *Nut Bilawal* is only known to experts. Its Poorvang is like 'Nut' and Uttarang is like Bilawal, is obcure Ma is Vadi. Stress is therefore, laid on its Poorvang and in this respect resembles with Nut. The Combination of Re and Dha is pleasant.

Jati—Wakra Sampoorna, *Vadi*—Ma, *Samvadi*—Sa, *Time*—Morning.

Aroh—SS, GMG, MPM, DNS.

Avaroh—SND, NP, MGMRS.

Pakad—SGGP, MGMRS.

15. *Nut Behag* is the Raga of Bilawal Thata and its nature resembles with that of Raga Nut, but at the time of singing Behag Ang is used in it.

16. *Nut Kamode*—It is also a form of Nut but if is sung in Kamode Ang.

17. *Nut Kedar* is also a form of Nut and is sung in Kedar Ang.

18. *Nut* is meant to excite warlike spirit by relating tales of bravery, and courage by warriors in song. Nut is different from Nut Bilawal, and is obscure, Ma is strong and is the Vadi. It is a mixture of Alhiya, Kamode and Chhaya. Stress is laid on the Poorvang, Dha and Ga, should be dropped in the Avaroh, and therefore, becomes different from Nut Bilawal.

The theory of Nut Behag, Kamode Nut, Kedar Nut and Nut Narain is included in Nut.

Jati—Wakra Sampoorna, *Vadi*—Ma, Samvadi Sa, *Time*—Night.

Aroh—S G M M, P M M M, P D N Ṡ.

Avaroh—Ṡ D N P, M P M G M, S R S.

Pakad—S R S, G M P M G M, S R S.

19. *Nut Narain* is a part of Nut Raga, with the exception that Dha is clealy shown in decent while Nee is weak in ascent.

20. *Behagra* is not known to all, but is a pretty melody fit for Thumri and for female voices in particular. It is a variety derived from Behaga, and like Behaga its Vadi is Ga. It is sung in Punjab. Both Ma, and both Nee, are used. The theories of Pat Behaga and Savani Behag resemble with the above.

Jati—Odava Sampoorna, *Vadi*—Ga, *Samvadi*—Nee, *Time*—Evening.

Aroh—Ṇ S. G M P, N Ṡ.

Avaroh—S Ṅ D P, N D P, M M G R S.

Pakad—Ṇ S, N D P, M G, M G R S.

21. *Pat Behag* is a kind of Rag Behagra and is sung in Behag Ang, Komal Nee is used and Re is used slightly in ascent, S N D is used repeatedly to increase beauty.

———

22. *Maloha* is obscure and is a mixture of 'Kedar' and 'Kamode' it is called Maloha Kedar, and is of comparatively modern invention. Its Vadi is Sa, and Nee should be pronounced clearly to distinguish it from Kedar. It should be sung in Bilampat rhythm.

Jati—Wakra Odave Sampoorna, *Vadi*—Sa, *Samvadi*—Pa, *Time*—Morning.

Aroh—M P N Ṡ, Ṙ Ṡ, G M P N Ṡ.

Avaroh—Ṡ N D P, M G M R S.

Pakad—S N D P, M P N S.

23. *Jaldhar* is also called the Jaldhar Kedar and is obscure and is also a variety of Kedar, Pa is Vadi, Ga is dropaed altogether. In kedar, Re, Nee and Dha are weak: but such is not the case in Jaldhar.

Jati—Shadava, *Vadi*—Ma, *Samvadi*—Sa, *Time*—Rainy Season.

Aroh—S R S, M R P P, D P M, N D Ṡ.

Avaroh—Ṡ N D P, M P M G M, S R S.

Pakad—M R P P, D P M R S.

24. *Durga* is only known to some experts, therefore, not at all popular. Its shastric name is Shudh Saveri, is obscure, Ma, is Vadi and Ga and Nee, are dropped both ways. It has a resemblance to Shudh Malhar and Sorath. Durga as sung today is different from the "Shudh Saveri" of olden days.

Jati—Odava, *Vadi*—Ma, *Samvadi*—Sa, *Time*—Noon.

Aroh—S R, M R, P D Ṡ.

Avaroh—Ṡ D P , D M R S.

Pakad—P D P, D M, M R S.

25. *Gunkali*—shastric name "Gandak Kadi" is an extremely pretty melody. It is obscure, Vadi is Sa, being an Uttarang its chief beauty is displayed in its Avaroh.

Jati—Sampoorna, *Vadi*—Sa, *Samvadi*—Pa, *Time*—Morning.

Aroh—S, G R P, N D Ṡ.

Avaroh—Ṡ N D P, G R S.

Pakad—G R S, N D N, R S.

26. *Pahadi* is very like Bhoopali, and takes the same scale, the Vadi marks the distinguishing feature. Easy styles may be sung in this in Bilampat rhythm and in the middle and lower scale. Dha and Nee are dropped, but Ma is inserted bringing a subtle change between Bhoopali and Pahadi, Vadi. being Sa, the Sa, Dha, combination is characteristic. Pahadi is popular in Punjab. There is Pahadi Jhinjoti also which takes Nee.

Jati—Odava, *Vadi*—Sa, *Samvadi*—Pa, *Time*—All time.

Aroh—S R G, P D Ṡ.

Avaroh—Ṡ D P, G R S D.

Pakad—S R G, P D P, G R S D.

27. *Mand* owes its origin to Marwar and Rajputana. It is a folk song of the people of Gujrat, and Kathiawar also, it is sung in various fascinating styles, also to a dance called Garba, in group song-dance by men and women. It should be rendered with a tremor to give the melody a characteristic touch. Sa, Ma, and Pa are strong Ma, is Vadi,

Jati—Wakra Sampoorna, *Vadi*—Sa, *Samvadi*—Pa, *Time*—All time.

Aroh—SGR, MG, P, MDP, NDS.

Avaroh—SD, NP, DM, PG, MR, GS.

Pakad—SGM, PM, G, PM, GS.

28. *Savani*—Bhat Khande has not given any classical description of this Raga. It is sung in Behaga Raga. It is one of the Ragas sung in Falgun month of Vikram Era.

29. *Raga Mulla or Mulla Kedar* is a Raga of Bilawal Thatā mixed with Kedar and also mixture of Rag Shiam and Kamode Re and Dha are not used in its ascent and Tivra and Madhyama are also used in it. Its movement is mainly done in medium and lower Octaves. It appears more lovely in Bilampat Laya.

Jati—Odava Sampoorna, *Vadi*—Sa, *Samvadi*—Ma, *Time*—Evening.
Aroh—NS, GMP, NS.
Avaroh—S, SNDP, MG, MRNS.
Pakad—RS, P, MP, NS.

30. *Chhaya* Raga originates in Bilawal Thatā. Some singers call it Chhaya Nut also but Nut and Chhaya are separate Ragas. Ga in ascent and Nee in descent are used in Nut but in Chhaya Nut Ga and Nee both remain in Wakra shape. Rest should be supposed similar to Chhaya Nut.

31. *Chhaya Tilak* is the other form of Chhaya which is made up of the mixture of Chhaya Nut and Tilak Kamode. RP, MG, SRGS notes of Tilak Kamode are used in it.
Movement of Notes—S, R, G, RG, MP, M, PG, SRG, MRG.

32. *Mewara* is a Raga of regional Folk song and drives its name from Folk songs sung in Mewar. The rules of classical songs do not play any prominent role in it.
Movement of Notes—M, GRG, S, RMPD, MP, MGRS.

33. *Pat Manjari* is obscure. These are two kinds of Pat Manjari. The other occurs in the Kafee Thatā. This Pat Manjari is also called Bengal. The Bilawal Ang is clearly shown. Its Vadi is Sa when sung in Bilampat laya and in middle and lower Octaves it is a beautiful classical melody and known only to few experts.

Jati—Sampoorna, *Vadi*—Sa, *Samvadi*—Pa, *Time*—Morning.
Aroh—SRS, NDNP, GRGMP.
Avaroh—MPNS, SND, MP, MGRS.
Paked—SGRG, MPMG, RS.

34. *Hansdhwani* is a Raga of Karnataka System and origonates in Bilawal Thatā. It is a Raga of Odava category. Ma and Dha are prohibited. Its vadi is Sa, but according to some singer's its Vadi is also Ga.

Jati—Odava, *Vadi*—Sa, *Samvadi*—Pa, *Time*—Night.

Aroh—SRGP, NS.
Avaroh—RS, N, D, GP, GRS.
Pakad—GRG, DN, GRRS.

35. *Deepak* is a Raga of Bilawal Thatā which is formed by the combination of Raga Behag and Jhanjhoti. Its movement is more in medium and lower Octaves. Re in ascent is prohibited while Dha is Wakra. The other form of Deepak is also in Khamaj Thatā but Deepak which is more popular is of Poorvi Thatā.

Jati—Shadava-Sampoorna, *Vadi*—Ga, *Samvadi*—Dha, *Time*—Night.
Aroh—G, GMP, NS.
Avaroh—S, ND, P, MGRS.
Pakad—GM, PMG, RS.

2

Khamaj Thata

Sa Re Ga Ma Pa Dha *Nee* Sa.

Khamaj is a Thata Vachak Raga. The old Shastric name of this Thata is Khambhoji deriving its name from King Kambhoj of Kambhoj (Cambay). *Nee* is Komal and rest of the notes are Shudh, hence it is the second step for beginners after Bilawal. It includes 17 Ragas of which 8 are more popular :—

Khamaj—Des—Tilak Kamode—Jejewanti—Jhanjhoti — Khambavati—Tilang—Durga Rageshari—Gara—Sorath—Naraini—Savant—Nagsuravali—Shudh Malhar — Partap Varali Tilak.

1. *Khamaj*		5. *Tilang*
2. *Des*		6. *Jhanjhoti*
3. *Tilak Kamode*		7. *Gara*
4. *Jejewanti*		8. *Sorath*

Khamaj and Des are excellent melodies for female Voices and for Thumari Style of Singing. Jhinjhoti and Gara lend themselves to get Toda style of playing on sitar. The secret of singing Tilak Kamode and Jejewanti is known to great musicians only.

1. *Khamaj* is the Thata Rag, and owes its origin to Cambay, (Kathiawar) re is dropped in the Aroh, *Nee*, plays an important part, Dha is prolonged in this way Ga Ma Dha-ma, Nee Dha Nee Sa. Its vadi Swara is Ga, This is extremely popular. It lends itself to

easy and difficult styles, particularly suited to female voices and in Thumri styles of singing.

Jati—Shadava Sampoorna, *Vadi*—Ga, *Samvadi*—Nee, *Time*—Night.

Aroh—SGMP, DNS,

Avaroh, SND, PMG, RS,

Pakad—S N D, M P, D M G.

2. *Des* is a very pretty melody and lends itself to all popular and easy styles, very suited to female voices, Thumari, is charming in Des, It is different to Deskar. There are delicate differences in Sorath and Des, to distinguish them from each other. Vadi is Pa and its peculiar tan is Ga, Re, Ga, Sa, both Ga, are inserted in the Avaroh, and this makes it differ from Sorath Viz: Nee, Dha Ma, Dha Ma, Ga Re, Ga Re Sa Nee Sa.

Jati—Odava Sampoorna, *Vadi*-Pa, *Samvadi*, Ra *Time*—Night,

Aroh—S R M P, N S.
Avaroh—SNDP, MG, RGS.

Pakad—R M P, N D P, P D P, M, G R G S.

3. *Tilak Kamode* lends itself to easy and diffcult style, suited to male and female voices, it is a dignified beautiful melody shows a tinge of 'Sorath' and Des, Dha is dropped in Aroh, and Re is Wakra Avaroh, The Ga, Sa, combination is its special feature. The pause on Nee, is peculiar, Re, is Vadi.

Jati—Shadava Sampoorna, *Vadi*—Re *Samvadi*, Pa, *Time*—Night
Aroh—S R G S, R M P D M P Ś,

Avaroh—S P D M G, S R G, S N,

Pakad—P N S R G, S, R, P M G, S N.

4. *Jejevanti* is appropriate for men's voices and may be termed as a parent Rag. It is, suited for heavy difficult styles like Dhurpad singing and on Been, Jejevanti is very important melody of the Khamaj Thata because Ga and Nee (Komal) are introduced, which points to the important fact that it heralds the approach of another Thata like Kafee, which takes Ga Nee (Komal). It is more or less obscure, Re is vadi, Both Ga, and both Nee, are used, This melody is a combination of Bilawal, Goud, and Sorath, Pa, Re, is its speciality. In Aroh, Ga, Nee, (Komal) are used. By inserting both Ga, it marks the approach to Kanhra.

Jati—Sampoorna, *Vadi*—Re, *Samvadi*, Pa, *Time*—Night
Aroh—SRR, RGRS, NDP, R, GMP, NS,

Avaroh—SNDP, DM, PRG, RS,

Pakad—R G R S, N D P, R,

5. *Jhinjhoti* a very popular pretty melody, more suited to female voices and easy light styles. Ga is vadi.

Jati—Sampoorna, *Vadī*—Ga, *Samvadi*, Nee, *Time*—All Time,

Aroh—D S, R M G, M P D N Ṡ.

Avaroh—S, N, D, P, M, G R S.

Pakad—D S, R M G, P, M G, R S, N, D P.

6. *Khambavati* is a very sweet melody suited to female voices, and to be sung in easy styles. It is not generally known, is more or less obscure. The difference between Khamaj and Khambavati, is this, that in Khambavati Re is inserted in Aroh, and its Aroh Avaroh, (ascent and descent) are wakra (crooked,) and the glide from Ma, to Sa, is very pleasant Ga, Ma, Sa is its specialty.

Jati—Shadava, *Vadi*—Ga, *Samvadi*—Dha, *Time*—Night,

Aroh—S R M P, D, P N Ṡ.

Avaroh—Ṡ, N D, P, D M, G M S.

Pakad—N, M P D P D S, N D P, D M, G M S.

7. *Tilang* is a very pretty melody, suited to female voices, particularly when the girls go to the wells to fetch water. There are beautiful water song compositions. Re, and Dha, are dropped both ways, Ga, is vadi. The mend, (glide) from Nee pa, is characteristic and extremely pleasing in this tune.

Jati—Odava, *Vadi*—Ga, *Samvadi*—Nee Time—Night.

Aroh—SGMPNṠ.

Avaroh ṠNPMGS.

Pakad—G M P, N P, N S, N P, G M G S.

8. *Durga* is prety melody and method of introdcing Tans in Sargam suits this Raga. If a slight tinge of re inserted, it would become Natki Ranjika, a shastric melody. There are 2 kinds of Durga, one occurs in Bilawal Thata and second in Khamaj Re and Pa in this is dropped both ways. Its vadi is Ga. This tune is obscure in the North and very popular in the South.

Jati—Odava, *Vadi*—Ga, *Samvadi*—Nee Time—Night

Aroh—SGMDNṠ.

Avaroh—ṠNDMGS.

Pakad G M S, R N D S, M G, M D, N D M G S.

9. *Rageshri* takes Ga (tivra), and Bageshri takes komal Ga, A Rag whose description is given exactly like Rageshri in the old Shastras is called 'Ravi Chandra' Rageshri, and is

obscure, while 'Bageshri' is extremely popular, Pa is dropped both ways, Ga is Vadi.

Jati—Shadava, *Vadi*—Ga, *Samvadi*—Nee *Time*—Night.

Aroh—SRS, GMD, NS.

Avaroh—SND, MG RS.

Pakad—R S, N D, S M G, M D N D, M G R S.

10. *Gara* is a very pretty melody and lends itself to easy styles of singing particularly for Gut Toda (a compostion for sitar) like Jhinjoti. In this melody the 'Madhya and 'Mandra' (middle and lower) Octave notes sound pleasing. It is invented by the Muslems. Re is Vadi, and like Jejevanti both Ga, and both Nee, are used.

Jati—Wakra Sampoorna, *Vadi*—Ga, *Samvadi*—Nee *Time*—All time.

Aroh—MPDNS, RGRGMP, DNS.
Avaroh—SNDNPMGRS, NS.

Pakad—RGRS, DNPDNS, GMRGRS.

11. *Sorath* is a very pretty melody suited for female voices to be sung in easy styles. Sorath is the name of a port in Kathiawar. Gazal, Thumari are charming in Des, and in Sorath, Ga, is dropped both ways. Its vadi is Re. In Aroh Re and Dha should be dropped. The mend from Ma Re, is its speciaity viz: Ma Re Ma Pa Nee Nee Sa, Re Sa Nee Dha, Pa, Dha, Ma, Re Re Re Nee Sa.

Jati—Odava Shadava *Vadi*—Re, *Samvadi*—Dha *Time*—Evening

Aroh —S, MRMP, NS.

Avaroh—SNDP, MRS.

Pakad—M R M P N S, N D P M R S.

12. *Narayani* is obscure. This melody is popular in the South and seems to be a variety of Sarang. Pratab Varali and Nag Soravi may be placed under Bilawal Thata also as both drop Nee, both ways, and take Ma. The tans (variations), resemble Khamaj however, though Nee is wakra and Ma, strong.

Jati—Odava Shadava *Vadi*—Re, *Samvadi*—Pa, *Time*—Night

Aroh—SR, MPDS.

Avaroh—SNDPMRS.

Pakad—SNDP, MPDP, MRDS.

13. *Savant* is more popular in the South. It has the same Avroh, as Asvari, but dha, is vadi in that Raga, while Ma is vadi, in Savan, Nee, is dropped both ways and ga in

Aroh. It is only known to some experts of the North.

Jati—Odava Sampoorna, *Vadi*—Ma, *Samvadi* Sa, *Time*—Morning.

Aroh—SRMPDS.

Avaroh—S D P M G R S.

Pakad—S R M M P D S D, M P P G R S.

14. *Nag Soravi* is obscure. This Raga could be placed under the Bilawal Thatā also. Like the former it drops Nee both ways. It is popular in the South and unknown in the North. These Southern Ragas are played at all times. They are Sargam Tans and do not take Alap (Sounds of the notes without pronouncing the notes).

Jati—Odava, *Vadi*—Ma, *Samvadi*—Sa, *Time*—All times.

Aroh—S G M P D S.

Avaroh—S D P M G S.
Pakad—P D S, G M G S.

15. *Shudh Malhar* is rendered only in Serious and difficult styles. It is suited for a man's voice. Malhar should be sung after Jejevanti. Shudh Malhar is obscure Ma is vadi and Ga Nee are dropped both ways. This Shudh Malhar is original pure Malhar from which the different varities of Malhar are derived.

Jati—Odava, *Vadi*—Ma, *Samvadi*—Sa, *Time*—Rainy Season.

Aroh—S R M P, M P, D S.

Avaroh—S D P, M R S.
Pakad—S R S, M M R P, M R S.

16. *Pratab Varali* is obscure and popular in South. Pratab Varali, Nag Soravali and Narayani, are similar and get distinct.

Jati—Odava Shadava, *Vadi*—Re, *Samvadi*—Pa, *Time*—Night.

Aroh—S R M P D S.

Avaroh—S D P M G R S.
Pakad—M G R, M P D, M P D S.

17. *Rag Tilak* is the *Raga* of Khamaj Thata. Dha is dropped in it.
Jati—Shadava, *Vadi*—Ga, *Samvadi*—Nee, *Time*—Night.

Aroh—S R G M, P N S.

Avaroh—S N P, M G R S.

Pakad—S R M P, M G R S.

3

Kafee Thata

Sa Re Ga Ma Pa Dha Nee Sa.

Kafee is a Thata Vachak Raga and its—Shastric name is Harpriya Mel. Most of the Ragas placed under this Thatā are to be rendered either at mid-day or at mid night. The kafee thata ragas are divided in to three groups i.e. Malhar, Kandra and Sarang, 45 Ragas are placed under this Thatā, out of which 16 are more popular :—

Kafee—Bageshri—Brindabani Sarang—Bhimplasi—Peelu—Gaudmalhar
Miankimalhar—Bahar—Sindhora—Sindhvi—Barva—Dhanasiri
Dhani—Pardeepki—Hanskankani—Plasi—Madhmad—Shudh Sarang
Budhans—Savant Sarang—Mianki Sarang—Lankdhan Sarang—Patmanjiri
Suba—Sughrai—Subasugrai—Shahana—Naikikandra—Decosakh
Kaunsikandra—Meghmalhar—Soordasi Malhar—Ramdasi Malhar
Nut Malhar—Meerabaiki Malhar—Chhajuki Malhar—Dhoolia Malhar
Roopmanjiri Malhar—Chanchal Malhar—Shiri Ranjini—Abhogi
Chanderkauns—Gaud—Husainikandra—Nilambari.

1. *Kafee*
2. *Bageshri*
3. *Bindrabani Sarang*
4. *Bheemplasi*
5. *Peelu*
6. *Gaud Malhar*
7. *Miyan ki Malhar*
8. *Bahar*
9. *Sindhora*
10. *Barva*
11. *Dhanashri*
12. *Shudh Sarang*
13. *Patmanjari*
14. *Nayki Kandra*
15. *Dev Shakh*
16. *Megh Malhar*

1. *Kafee* is a Hori type of Raga and all the melodies are very sweet and are used in Dhrupad, Dhamar and Khyal Gaykees by the expert musicians.

Kafee is the Thata Rag. and is so popular that it is sung in all styles and played on all instruments and the Thata is named after it, Pa is Vadi, Ga & Nee are komal, in Kafee, but experts introduce Ga and Nee tivra, with such cleverness in the Aroh, that it lands additional charm, Nee is the note of Nyas (restful emotion), Sa, Ga, Pa, form the chief combination.

Jati—Sampoorna. *Vadi*—pa, *Samvadi*—Sa, *Time*—Mid night.

Aroh—S R G, M, P, D N S.

Avaroh—S N D, P, M G, R, S.

Pakad—S S, R R, G G, M M, P.

2. *Bageshri* is a popular beautiful melody specially for female voices. Shri Ranjini is another melody which is generally confused with Bageshri. Shri Ranjini drops pa, while Bageshri, retains it in Avaroh. Then again Bageshri takes both Ga, in the famous Tarana of Bahadur Sen who was a great musician. Shri Ranjini keeps clear of Ga tivra, Re Pa, are dropped in Aroh only, Ma is Vadi, Pa should not be emphasized in Avaroh, otherwise it will look like Dhanashri.

Jati—Shadava Sampoorna, *Vadi*—Ma, *Samvadi* Sa, *Time*—Mid Night.

Aroh—S N D N S, M G, M D N S.

Avaroh— S, N D, M P M G R S.

Pakad—S, N D, S, M D N D, M, G R, S.

3. *Brindabani Sarang* is favourite among experts, Dha and Ga, are dropped altogether. It is a beautiful melody. Dha can be used carefully in Avaroh as a wakra.

Jati—Odava Odava, *Vadi*—Re, *Samvadi*—Pa, *Time*—Mid day.

Aroh—N S, R, M P, N S.

Avaroh—S N P, M R, S.

Pakad—N S R, M R, P M R, S.

4. *Bheempalasi* is as popular as Peelu and in Yaman Kaliyan. Ma, is Vadi, and Re Dha, are dropped in Aroh.

Jati—Odava Sampoorna, *Vadi*—Ma, *Samvadi*—Sa, *Time*—Mid day.

Aroh—N S G M, P, N S.

Avaroh—S N D P M, G R S.

Pakad—N S M, M G, P M, G, M G R S.

5. *Peelu* stands by itself. It is an important popular melody Bhajans are appealing in Peelu. The correct way of singing Peelu is by the descendents of Tan Sen. It is an invention of Muslim Gunis. It is a Raga of Sankeern jati and mixture of Bhairavi Bheemplasi & Gauri.   All the 12 notes can be used in this melody.

Jati—Sampoorna. *Vadi*—Ga, *Samvadi*—Nee, *Time*—Mid day.

Aroh—N S C, R G, M P, D P. N D P, S.

Avaroh—N D P G, N S.

Pakad—N S G N S, P D N D S, N S.

6. *Goud Malhar* is a melody of Kafee Thata, the other type is placed under the Khamaj Thata. Being seasonal the theme of the melody is always that of the seasonals occasion, this is peculiar to all seasonal songs. It is beautiful and classical, suited for female voices.   There are some extremely fascinating compositions by Gunis.

All Malhars should be sung at all times during monsoon, the compositions generally treat rainy weather.   Goud Malhar is more popular than Shudh Malhar.

Jati—Sampoorna, *Vadi*—Ma, *Samvadi*—Sa, *Time*—Monsoon Season.

Aroh—S R M, P, D S.

Avaroh—S N P, M P, G M, R S.

  or—R G R M G R S, R P, M P, D S.

Avaroh—S D N P M, G M R S.

Pakad—R G R, M G R S, P M P D S, D P M,

7. *Mian ki Malhar* is an extremely beautiful and clever blend of Kanhra and Malhar. It is heavy, and classical, and is the invention of Tan Sen, of the reign of Emperor Akbar. It should only be rendered in the most difficult styles by male voices in Bilampat, always beginning from Mandra Sthan (lower scale).   Miyan ki Malhar, is heiriditory in the family of Tan Sen, Sa is Vadi, Ga, is tremulous, this fact is significant of Kanhra, and the combination of Ma, Re, Pa, points to the Malhar Ang. Ma, is enforced, Nee, Dha, Nee, Pa are also prominent. Its special Tan is, Re, Ma Re Sa, Nee Pa, Ma Pa, Nee Dha, Nee Sa, Ma Re, Pa, Nee Dha, Nee, Sa, Pa Ga Ma Re Sa. Both Nee, are used occasionally, one after the other.

Jati—Sampoorn Shadava, *Vadi*—Sa, *Samvadi*—Pa, *Time*—Monsoon.

Aroh—R M R S, M R, P, N D N S.

Avaroh—S N P, M P, G M R S.

Pakad—R M R S, N P, M P, N D, N S' P, G M R S.

8. *Bahar* is a most exquisite seasonal melody, and a Mishra Mel, (mixture) of Bageshri, Malhar and Adana, sounds well in Drut Lay (fast speed) also. Bahar lends itself to harmonise with other melodies so that there are combinations like Hindole Bahar, Malkauns, Bahar, and Bhairava Bahar, Ma, is Vadi, Re is dropped in Aroh and Dha is dropped in Avroh.

Jati—Shadava Shadav, *Vadi*—Ma, *Samvadi*—Sa, *Time*—Mid night.
Aroh—N S, G M, P G M, D, N S,

Avaroh—S, N P M P, G M, RS.

Pakad—M P G M, D, N S.

9. *Sindhora* drops Ga Nee in Aroh, like Gunkali etc. Sa, is Vadi. It is a light pretty melody.
Jati—Odava Sampoorna, *Vadi*—Sa, *Samvadi*—Pa, *Time*—Night.
Aroh—S R M P D S,
Avaroh—S N D P M G R S.
Pakad—S R G R S, R M P, D S; R G R S.

10. *Rag Sindhavi* or Sindh is also called Sindhora all Particulers resemble with that of Sindhavi. Both Ga are used and Re is Strong.
Movement of notes—N D H, R, G M G, R, S, M G R, N S N, P D N.

S, G, G, M, M, G G R, S, M G R, N S N, P D N S.

11. *Barva* is invented by Muslems, Re is Vadi, both Nee, Re and Dha are used. It resembles with Desi a bit, and should be more popularized.
Jati—Shadava Sampoorna, *Vadi*—Re, *Samvadi*—Pa,—*Time*—Midday.

Aroh—S R M P D N S,
Avaroh—S N D P, D M G R G S.
Pakad—G R G S, R P G R G S, M P S, N D P D M G R G S.
One type of Barva is also called Punjabi Barva resembling in theory with Barva.
12. *Dhanashri* is a lovely classical melody, and similar to Bheempalasi, Dhanashri takes Pa as Vadi, and Pa Ga, is the Chief combination. Bheempalasi, takes Ma, as Vadi and Ma Ga, is the chief combination. If Sa, is made Vadi it creates Dhanashri. One type of Dhanashri is also used in Bhairava Thata.
Jati—Odava Sampoorna, *Vadi*—Pa, *Samvadi*—Sa, *Time*—Midday.
Aroh—N S G N P N S,
Avaroh—S N D P M G R S,
Pakad—P P, G P, G M G, R S, N S.

13. *Dhani* Ga is Vadi, Re Dha, are dropped both ways, Sa Ma Ga. form a combination.
Jati—Odava, *Vadi*—Ga, *Samvadi*—Nee, *Time*—Midday.
Aroh—N S G, M P, N S.

Avaroh—S N, P, M G, S.
Pakad—N S G G, S S M P, N N P M N G, M P G S.

14. *Pardeepaki* or *Patdeepki* is quite obscure. Ga Dha, are dropped in Aroh, Sa, is Vadi, Re is extremely weak. Both Ga, are used. After Sarang. Patmanjiri should be sung and after that, Pardeepaki should be sung. These melodies are known only to some experts.

Jati—Odava Sampoorna, *Vadi*—Sa, *Samvadi*—Pa, *Time*—Evening.

Aroh—G S G M P N S.

Avaroh—S N D P M G R S.

Pakad—P P, G, R S R N S, S G M P N S, G R S N D P.

15. *Hans Kankani* is very attractive Re and Dha are dropped in Aroh, Pa, is Vadi Both Ga and Nee are used affectively. The combination of Sa Ma Pa, is strong.

Jati—Odava Sampoorna, *Vadi*—Pa, *Samvadi*—Sa, *Time*—Midday.

Aroh—N S G, M P N S.

Avaroh—S N D P, M G R S.

Pakad—G M P, M P, G R S, M P N S N D P.

16. *Plasi* is mixture of Plasi and Bheem Ragas and is used to sing songs and Bhajans. It is a Jati Gan. Dha is prohibited. The theory resembles with that of Dhanas shri

Jati—Shadava, *Vadi*—Pa, *Samvadi*—Sa, *Time*—Midday.

17. *Madhmadh* is generally sung as Sarang. Ga Dha, are dropped. Re is Vadi.

Jati—Odava *Vadi*—Re, *Samvadi*—Pa, *Time*—Midday.

Aroh—S R G M P, N S

Avaroh—S N P. M R S.

Pakad—N N S R M R, S N P, M P, M R, S N S.

18. *Shudh Sarang* drops Ga, but takes Dha, freely. All Sarangs are bright midday melodies. They differ from each other by clever manipulations of *Ga*, Dha and *Nee*. Such delicate distinctions are only restricted to great experts.

Jati—Odava Shadava, *Vadi*—Re, *Samvadi*—Pa, *Time*—Mid day.

Aroh—S R M P N S.

Avaroh—S D N P, M, R S.

Pakad—S R M R, P M P D P, N S, R N P, M R S.

19. *Bud Hans* is unknown in the North but is popular in the South. Bud Hans is sung in two-ways, with Nee tirva and Nee komal. It is a variety of Sarang therefore Ga, is dropped, Its Vadi is Re, and Ma should be made clear. Bud Hans is obscure generally but known in the Punjab. It a is most attractive melody.

Jati—Shadava, *Vadi*—Re, *Samvadi*—Pa, *Time*—Mid day.

Aroh—S R M P, D N P, N S.

Avaroh—S N P, D P, M R S.

Pakad—N N P M, P N P M, R S.

20. *Savant Sarang* is a midday melody, in this Raga Ga and Dha are droped in Aroh and in Avaroh only Ga is dropped. Re is Vadi.

Jati—Odava Shadava, *Vadi*—Re, *Samvadi*—Pa, *Time*—Mid day.

Aroh—S R M P N S.

Avaroh—S N D P, M P R S.

Pakad—R S M R M P, N D P M P R S, N S

21. *Miyan ki Sarang* is invented by Tan Sen, and popular among the Senya Gharana. It is a serious melody and should be emphasized in the middle and lower notes. The word Miyan indicates Tan Sen, and is dedicated to him.

Jati—Shadava, *Vadi*—Re, *Samvadi* Pa, *Time*—Mid day.

Aroh—S R M P, D P, N D, N S.

Avaroh—S N P, D N D P, M P M R S.

Pakad—S R M P, M R, S N D N S.

22. *Lankdhadhan Sarang* drops Dha both ways. Both Nee, are used. Re, is Vadi. It is something like Des. Both Ga, are introduced and yet it is a variety of Sarang. It is a lovely melody, and should be popularised.

Jati—Shadava, *Vadi*—Re, *Samvadi*—Pa, *Time*—Mid day.

Aroh—P N S R G R, M P N S.

Avaroh—S N P G, M R S.

Pakad—P, N S R R S, N P, M P N S.

23. *Pat Manjari* Should be sung after Sarang and the clever use of Ga, Dha, should distinguish from Sarang and Des. In Aroh, Ga Dha, are weak, therefore it takes shape of Sarang. But both Nee, are used. It is obscure. Sa, is Vadi.

Jati—Odava Sampoorna, *Vadi*—Sa, *Samvadi*—Pa, *Time*—Mid day.

Aroh—S R M P N S.

Avaroh—S N D P, M G R S.

Pakad—S R M P, N D P, M R G R N S.

24 *Suha* is a Purva Ang midday melody. It is the counterpart of Adana which is Uttar ang. Suha drops dha, Adana retains dha. Ma, is Vadi. Its Purva takes Ga, but Uttar takes Sarang. The Nee, Pa, is charming. The rest on ma, completes the harmony.

Jati—Shadava, *Vadi*—Ma, *Samvadi*—Sa, *Time*—Mid day.

Aroh—S R G M P N S.

Avaroh—S N P M, G R S.

Pakad—M R N P, G M P N, N P M P, G M R S.

25. *Sughrai* is the counterpart of Shahana, and retains the Sarang Ang in Aroh, Dha is dropped in Aroh. In Adana Dha, is komal. In Shahana, Dha is shudha. These melodies are alike and yet different. The Tar Sthan (Upper Octave) Sa, is charming, Pa, is Vadi.

Jati—Shadava Sampoorna, *Vadi*—Pa, *Samvadi* Sa, *Time*—Mid day.

Aroh—S R G M P N S.

Avaroh—S N D P, M G R S.

Pakad—N S, G M R M P, G N, N D P, M R M P, G M R S.

26. *Suha Sughrai* is a mixture of Suha & Sughrai. Particulars resemble with that of Sughrai.

27. *Shahana* is a new kind of melody, and like Adana, Durbari and Megh it is an invention of the Muslim musicians. It is a heavy classical obscure melody. A slight tinge of Dha, in Avaroh, distinguishes it from Adana. It takes *Ga*, therefore, it differs from Sarang also.

Jati—Shadava Sampoorna, *Vadi*—Pa, *Samvadi* Sa, *Time*—Mid night.

Aroh—S R G M, P N S.

Avaroh—S N D P, M P, G R S.

Pakad—D P M P S N P, G M P, G M R.

28. *Naiki Kandra* is a mixture of 'Kosi' and 'Bageshri, Dha, is dropped. Both Nee, are used, Ma is Vadi In Purva Ang, it is like Suha. In Uttar it is like Sarang.

Jati—Shadava, *Vadi*—Ma, *Samvadi*—Sa, *Time*—Mid night.

Aroh—S R G M, P G, S.

Avaroh—S G, P M, G R S.

Pakad—N P M P, G N P G S, N P G M R S.

29. *Deosakh* or Deshakh is a mixture of Kanhra and Megh, and is like Suha, Pa is vadi. Both Nee, are used. Dha, Ga are weak. Sa, is tremulous and it retains the Sarang Ang.

Jati—Shadava Sampoorna, *Vadi*—Pa, *Samvadi*—Sa *Time*—Mid day.

Aroh—S R M, P N̊ S

Avaroh—S N D P, M G, R S

Pakad—N S R M, D P N D G S, N D P S, N, G M R S

30. *Kosi Kandara* is obscure and only known to gunis, It is a mixture of Malkaus and Dhanashri. In Aroh, Re is dropped It should be more popularised.

Jati—Shadava Sampoorna, *Vadi*—Ma, *Samvadi*—Sa, *Time*—Night.

Aroh—N S, G M, P M, D N S.

Avaroh—S N D M, P M, G R S.

Pakad—S N D M P, G M R S.

31. *Megh Malhar* is one of the great God tunes, excites thunder and lightening in nature. It is to be sung by men and in difficilt styles rendering the Gamak in such a way so as to make them sound like thunder. It is grave, dignified and a favourite with artists. It should be sung in Bilampat Rhythm, in Madh and Tar Sthan, Ga, Dha, are dropped both ways, Re is tremulous, Ma, Re, form a strong combination, Sa, is Vadi.

Jati—Odava, *Vadi*—Sa, *Samvadi*—Pa, *Time*—Monsoon.

Aroh—S R M P, N S.

Avaroh—S N P, M R S.

Pakad—S N P N S R M R S, N P M P, S, N S

32. *Surdasi Malhar* is the invention of the Asectic poet Surdas, in the time of Emperor Akbar, and owes its name after him. It drops Ga Dha, in Aroh, and takes Nee, tivra, in its Avaroh. The introduction of Ga, Dha, in Avaroh, makes it distinct from 'Sarang' Ma, Re, makes it look like Sorath, but in Sorath, Dha, is pronounced Sohs and Adana both give prominence to Ga, therefore. Surdasi becomes different. Surdasi, is a mixture of Malhar and Madh Madh, Ma, is Vadi.

Jati—Odava Sampoorna, *Vadi*—Ma, *Samvadi*—Sa, *Time*—Seasonal.

Aroh—S R M P N S.

Avaroh—S N P M, N D P, M R S.

Pakad—S R M P M, N D P, N S, N D P G M, R S.

33. *Ramdasi Malhar* was invented by the expert Ramdas, in the reign of Emperor Akbar. Both Nee, and Ga, are used. There are 12 Malhars that may be placed the Kafee Thata. Three Malhars come under the Khamaj Thata, Experts know the secret of each.

Jati—Sampoona, *Vadi*—Ma, *Samvadi*—Sa, *Time*—Monsoon.

Aroh—N S R, G M, P G M, N P N S.

Avaroh—S N D N P, G M R S.

Pakad—S R G M P, G M P, N P, D N S.

34. *Nut Malhar* is an obscure Raga. The different varieties of Malhars with their subtle technicalities are known only to the few great experts. They are all difficult. Nut and Goud, are similar to each other, but the Pakad, (catch), shows the difference, the secret of performing them is known to the gunis (experts). In Nut Malhar, Ma, is Vadi. Its peculiarity is Ma, Re, Pa, Pa, Dha, Nee. Its Aroh is wakra (crooked) Ga, Ma, are always rendered together viz : Ga Ma Pa, Ga Ma Re, and so on to point out its special feature. The Dha and Nee Goud Malhar should be touched lightly, while in Nut Malhar, they are shown clearly and dwelt upon at lenght, so as to illustrate them fully.

Jati—Sampoorna, *Vadi*—Ma, *Samvadi*—Sa, *Time*—Rainy season.

Aroh—S R G M, R P, M P D N S.

Avaroh—S N D P M G, M R S

Pakad—S R G M, G P M G R S S N S.

35. *Mirabai Ki Malhar* was invented by the famous ascetic poetess Queen of Mewar Mirabai, who composed Bhajans (hymes) and performed worship in the temple of Chittor, dedicated to her sacred name. It is a mixture of Adana and Malhar. The secret of introducing both Ga, Dha and Nee, is known to the experts. Mirabai Bhajans are full of spiritual feeling. Both Ga and both Dha are used.

Jati—Wakra Shadava Sampoorna, *Vadi*—Ma, *Samvadi*—Sa, *Time*—Night.

Aroh—N S R M R P, N D N S.

Avaroh—S D N P, N P, G M P G M R S.

Padak—M R, P M N P, D N P, G M R, S R S.

36. *Charji Ki Malhar* originates from Kafee Thatā. The combination of Mand Re in Purvang and that of S N D P, G R in Uttarang make it specially more clear.

Jati—Wakra Shadava Sampoorn, *Vadi*—Ma, *Samvadi*—Sa, *Time*—Night.

Aroh—S M R M P, N D S.

Avaroh—S N D P, G R, R G S.

Pakad—S N D P G R.

37. *Dhulya Malhar* is of Kafee Thatā. The combination of Ma Re is like that of Chanchal ki Malhar. The movement in wakra appears more sweet.

Jati—Wakra Shadava Sampoorna, *Vadi*—Ma, *Samvadi*—Sa, *Time*—Night.

Aroh—S R M P, N D S.

Avaroh—S R S, N D P, M R S.

Pakad—M S, N D P, M R, M M P.

38. *Roop Manjiri Malhar* is of **Kafee Thatā and Malhar Ang. Both Ga are used**

in it. The combination of M R & R P makes the nature a Raga more clear and use of M G M R in Purvang more sweet.

Jati—Wakra Shadava Sampoorna, *Vadi*—Ma, *Samvadi*—Sa, *Time*—Night.
Aroh—S, M R P, N D S.

Avaroh—S N D P. M R M G S.

Pakad—N D N P, M R M, G S.

39. *Chanchal's Malhar* originates in Kafee Thatā and resembles more with Charjir ki Malhar. M R, G G, M R S movement of notes appears more sweet.

Jati—Wakra Shadav Sampoorna, *Vadi*—Ma, *Samvadi*—Sa, *Time*—Night.
Aroh—S M R, R P, M P S.
Avaroh—S N P, M P, R M S R S.

Pakad—N S, R, N S, P N M P.

40. *Shri Ranjini* is as lovely as Bageshri. It is Shastric. Pa, is dropped and Ga (komal) is used. Bageshri and Shri Ranjini are confused by the singers while in practice.

Jati—Odava Shadava, *Vadi*—Ma, *Samvadi*—Sa, *Time*—Mid Night.
Aroh—S G M D N S.
Avaroh—S N D M G R S.
Pakad—N S, M G M D, N D M G R S.

41. *Abhogi* is a Raga of Southern System but is used in Hindustani System also. It is the Raga of Kafee Thata. Its vadi is Sa, Pa and Nee are prohibited.

Jati—Odava, *Vadi*—Sa, *Samvadi*—Ma, *Time* Eventing.
Aroh—SRG, MDS.

Avaroh SD, M, G Rs.

Pakad—M G, M D, S.

42. *Chandar Kauns* is a Raga of Kafee Thata. The movement in lower and medium Octaves i.e. in S, N D M D N S; M G S. makes it more clear. Re and Pa are dropped.

Jati—Odava, *Vadi*—Sa, *Samvadi*—Ma, *Time*—Evening.
Aroh—S G M, D N S,

Avaroh—S N D M G R S.

Pakad—M D N S, M G S.

43. *Gaud* originates in Kafee Thata and is mixture of Kandra in Purvang and of Malhar Ang in Uttarang.

Jati—Sampoorna, *Vadi*—Pa, *Samvadi*—Sa, *Time* Evening

Aroh—N S, G M R P, D P S.

Avaroh—S D N P, M P, M R S.

Pakad—P, M P G, M R S.

44. *Huseini Kanhra* begins with Ma like Adana. The Kanhra Ang (form) is more evident in Huseini than is in Adana. The Sarang Ang is also evident in Adana, Huseini, Suha, Sughrai, Sur Malhar and Megh. The high SN Sounds very pleasant. The Kanhra. Sarang, Malhar and Kafee groups are like each other. But the clever manipulation of Dha Ga in all these melodies mark the individual charactristic.

Great care should be taken to reader each Raga in its own purity.

Jati—Sampoorna, *Vadi*—Sa, *Samvadi*—Pa. *Time*—night

Aroh—S R G, M P N s.

Avaroh S N D P. M P. G R S.

Pakad—M P D N s, G M R S.

45. *Neelambari* is modern, Pa is Vadi Ga is rendered with Kunpat (shake) It is very charming Melody.

Jati—Sampoorna, *Vadi* Da, *Samvadi* Sa, *Time* Day

Aroh—S R G, M P, N S

Avaroh—Ś, N D P M G R S.

Pakad—P P D P, M G M P, G R N S.

4

Asawari Thata

Sa Re Ga Ma Pa *Dha Nee* Sa

The shastric name of Asawari is Bhairavi and in Shastric period it was sung with Re tivra. Asawari is now a thata vachak Raga. In times of Raga-Ragini system Asawari was considered as the ragini of Shri Raga. Asawari is a mystic melody and has power over the super natural forces. 16 Ragas are placed under this Thata, out of them 6 are more popular :

Asawari-Jonpuri—Darbari Kandra—Adana—Desi—Komaldesi—Gandhari— Devgan dhari—Khut—Khut Todi—Jangula—Zeelaf—Gopiki Basant—Mundrick Kandra — Sindh-bhairvi—Abhiri·

1. *Asawari*	4. *Adana*
2. *Jonpuri*	5. *Gandhari*
3. *Darbari Kandra*	6. *Sindh Bhairavi*

The haunting Asawari has deep facination for peacocks and serpants completely subjugating them paralyzing and hypnotising their will. All the Ragas in this Thata are very sweet melodies and attract the audience.

1. *Asawari*, is the Thata Raga extremely popular, beautiful and mystic, suited to male and female voices. The correct way is Re, tivra, in the Aroh, and Avaroh.

Jati—Odava Sampoorna, *Vadi*—Dha *Samvadi* Ga, *Time*—Morning.

Aroh—S R M P, D S.

Avaroh—S, N, D, P, M G G, R S.

Pakad—R, M, P, N, D, P.

2. *Jonpuri*, is a mixture of Madh Mad and Asawari. It was invented by Sultan Husein of Jounpur, and named after the city. Jonpuri, is confused with Asawari.

Jati—Shadava Sampoorna, *Vadi*—Dha, *Samvadi*—Ga, *Time*—Morning.

Aroh—S R M, P, D, N S,

Avaroh— S, N D, P M G R S.

Pakad—M P, N D P. M P G, R M P.

3. *Durbari Kandra* is the invention of Tan Sen, and is a grand impressive dignified melody only to be sung in the most difficult styles by male voices, and on the Rudra Been. It was sung in the mighty Emperor Akbar's Court, hence called Durbari. The Tana, (expansion) in the Mandra Saptak (lower Octave) is its characteristic, Nee, Pa, form the main combination, and Ga, is Andolit, (swings and is tremulous). Kanhra, originally means Karnat. The word Kanhra, came into vogue during Muslim regime. It lends itself to endless variations over a great range. Durbari, commands respect.

Jati—Sampoorna Shadava, *Vadi*—Re *Samvadi*—Pa, *Time*—Night.

Aroh— N S, R G, R S, M P D, N S.

Avaroh—S D N P, M P G, M R, S,

Pakad—G R R S, D N S, R S.

4. *Adana*, heralds the approach of morning Raga, hence it should be sung before the morning melodies. Its Shastric name is *Athana*, and known as such in the South. The Tans (variations) in the Madhya and Tar Saptakas, are extremely pleasant. Ga is dropped in Aroh, Ga, Ma Re, combination is repeated over and over again. Nee Pa, makes it look like Sarang.

The Pa, Ga, combination in Avaroh, distinguishes it from Sarang. This secret is known to Experts. Adana is a lovely tune and quite popular.

Jati—Shadava, *Vadi*—Sa, *Samvadi*—Pa, *Time*—Mid Night.

Aroh—SRMP, DNS.

Avaroh—S D N P, M P, G M R S,

Pakad—S D N S, D N P, M P, G M R S.

5. *Desi* is known only to the experts. The Purva Ang (1st half) is like 'Sarang' and the Uttar Ang (2nd half), is like Asavari. It is a heavy melody and lends itself to serious styles. Ga, Dha, are dropped in Aroh, the Re, Nee. combination is characteristic and pleasant. Ga, is tremulous. Desi, is different from Des and Deskar.

Jati—Odava Sampoorna, *Vadi*—Pa, *Samvadi*—Re, *Time*—Morning.

Aroh—S R, M P N S

Avaroh—S N D P, M G R S.

Pakad—S D P M M, P D M G R S, R N S.

6. *Komaldesi*—The Theory of Desi also applies with Komal Desi.

7. *Gandhari* Asavari and Dhanashri, are most exquisitely blended in this melody. The Dhanashri Ang, is apparent in the Aroh and Asavari Ang, in the Avaroh. It is a Raga which is only known to the experts and sung in heavy styles more suited to male voices. Gandhari is a wonderful melody.

Jati—Odava Sampoorna, *Vadi*—Dha, *Samvadi*—Ga, *Time*—Morning

Aroh—S R M P N S.

Avaroh—S N D P M G R S.

Pakad—M P N D P, P P G M P, G R S.

8. *Devgandhari* In Devagandhari both Ga and Nee can be used.

9. *Khut* in Sanskrit means 6, hence Khut is a Mishr Mel (mixture) of 6 Ragas. It is a bright obscure melody and with gamak (Gitakari) Tans (variations). Experts introduce both the Re, Ga, Dha and Nee, with extremes cleverness showing the Swarup (form) of Bhairava in its Purva Ang and Asawri, in its Uttar Ang.

Jati—Shadava Sampoorna, *Vadi*—Dha, *Samvadi*—Ga, *Time*—Morning.

Aroh—P S, G M, P D N S.

*Avaroh—*Ṡ N D P, D M G R S.

*Pakad—*Ṡ N D P, D M, G R S.

10. *Khut Todi.* In Khut Todi some singers take Pancham as Vadi note.

11. *Jangula* is used to sing Thumary, Tappa and Gazals. Both Dha are used in it. One type of Jangula is popular in Thata Asawari while the other in Bhairava. It is free from classical bindings. It can be recoganized by the movement of notes only. Its vadi is Pa.

*Movement of notes—*G R G S, R M, P, D N D, P, D, M P, R G R S, R M P.

12. *Jeelaf* is an Arabic & Persian word and owes its origin in Muslem period by Amir Khusaro. One type of Jeelaf is used in Thata Asawari while the other in Bhairava. It is formed by the combination of Jonpuri & Khut.

*Jati—*Odava Sampoorna, *Vadi—*Dha, *Samvadi—*Ga, *Time—*Day.

*Aroh—*N S, G, M, P, P M, P D N Ṡ.

*Avaroh—*R N Ṡ, D P, G P M G R S.

*Pakad—*N S, G M P, G R S.

13. *Gopika Basant* originates from Thata Asawari. It is the Raga of Wakra Category and Re is prohibited. It is sung mainly in Southern India.

*Jati—*Shadava, *Vadi—*Sa, *Samvadi—*Pa, *Time—*Morning.
*Aroh—*S G M P, D, D N S.

*Avaroh—*S, D N, D M, P, G, G M S.

*Pakad—*M P G, M G S.

14. *Raga Mundareek Kandra* is the Raga of Asawari Thata and is of mixed Category. Hindol in ascent and Darbari Kandra in discent are used in it.

*Jati—*Odava Shadava, *Vadi—*Re, *Samvadi—*Pa, *Time—*Night.

*Aroh—*S G, M D N D.

*Avaroh—*Ṡ, P, Ṡ D, N P, M G M R S.

*Pakad—*M D, N D, N P, M P, M G R S.

15. *Sindh Bhairavi* owes its origin in Thata Asawari. Both Re are used in it. Some singers sing in Bhairavi Ang. Its movement is mainly in lower and medium Octaves.

*Jati—*Sampoorna, *Vadi—*Dh- *Samvadi—*Ga, *Time—*All Time.

Aroh—S R N S, R G M P, D N S.

Avaroh—S N D P, M G R S.

Pakad—R N S, D P D M, P G R N S, D P D M, P G R S

16. *Abheeri* is obscure. It is so lyrical that with the accompaniment of flute it is fit for dancing. It gives an impression of Bheemplasi but Bheemplasi takes Dha tivra where as Abheeri takes Dha Komal. It is an enquisitely beautiful melody.

Jati—Odava Sampoorna, *Vadi*—Ma, *Samvadi*—Nee, *Time*—Moining.

Aroh—S G M P N S.

Avaroh—S N D P M G Ṙ S

Pakad—M P Ṡ N D P G M P D P GM G R S.

5

Bhairavi Thata

Sa Re Ga Ma Pa *Dha Nee* Sa

Bhairavi is a Thata Vachak Raga and Shastric name of this Raga is Todi but the raga is popularly known as Bhairavi. At the time of Raga Ragini System it was the ragini of Bhairva Raga. The Ragas placed under this Thata are 12, out of which *Bhairavi andMal Kauns* are more popular.

Bhairavi—Malkauns. Bilaskhani—Todi—Komal Bageshri Bhoopalitodi—Basantmukhari—Motaki—Uttargunkali—Dhanashiri—Asawari—Mudrakee—Sarvari.

The melodies of remaining Ragas are Sweet and charming but are not common in-practice.

1. *Bhairavi* is the Thata Raga, with notes komal, it is most popular for female voices and Thumri, style. Being Sampooran, it can be rendered with expansions in 3 Octaves, and various Tals with full effect. Dhurpad, and Khyal, are rare in Bhairavi. Some expert singers introduce Re, shudha for additional charm. Vadi, is Ma.

Jati—Sampoorna, *Vadi*—Ma, *Samvadi*—Sa, *Time*—Morning.

Aroh—S, R, G, M, P, D, N, S.

Avaroh—S, N, D, P, M, G, R, S.

Pakad—M R, S R S, D N S.

2. *Malkauns* is one of the 6 great God tunes, to be rendered in the classical styles, at midnight. It is most popular, suited for male voices. It is Odava takes 5 notes komal.

There is another classical God tune. Hindole, which is also Odava, takes 5 notes. The difference in the 2 Ragas is great. One is mystic, full of deep feelings, while Hindole, is a bright melody full of hopes fit for male voices. Re, Pa, is dropped in both melodies.

Jati—Odava, *Vadi*—Ma, *Samvadi*—Sa, *Time*—Night.

Aroh—N, S, G, M, D, N S.

Avaroh—S N D, M G, M G S.

Pakad—M G, M D N D, M G S.

3. *Bilaskhani Todi* was invented by the son of Tan Sen, and called after his name. It is a heavy serious melody to be rendered in the most difficult styles, known only to experts. The Re, Nee, combination is striking Pa, is weak. Bilaskhani Todi, retains the purity, in the family of Tan Sen up to now. Although it takes the notes of Bhairavi, the method of rendering it is like Todi. This secret is known to experts.

Jati—Wakra Sampoorna, *Vadi*—Dha, *Samvadi*—Ga, *Time*—Morning.

Aroh—S, R G R, M G, P D N S.

Avaroh—S, N D P, D M G R, G M G R S.

Pakad—S R N D N S R G M G R S.

4. *Komal Bageshri* is different to Bageshri. It is a combination of Bageshri and Todi, a difficult melody and only to be rendered by the experts in heavy classical styles. When a Raga is so unknown there is difference of opinion even among the experts about it and one should always be guided by the existing practices. Both Dha, are used in Avaroh, and Re, is weak in Aroh.

Jati—Shadava Sampoorn, *Vadi*—Pa, *Samvadi*—Sa, *Time*—Morning.

Aroh—N S, G M P D N S.

Avaroh—S D, N D P, M G R S.

Pakad—N S G M P D N S, P D G R S.

5. *Bhoopal Todi* takes the same notes as Bhoopali, Re, Ga, Dha, are komal, and placed under the Bhairavi Thata as a morning melody while in Bhoopali, Re, Ga, Dha, are tivra, and placed under the Kalian Thata as an evening melody. Bhoopal, is the counterpart of Bhoopali. Bhoopal, is very popular. Ma, Nee are dropped both ways. The Pa, Ga, combination is peculiar.

Jati—Odava, *Vadi*—dha, *Samvadi*—Ga, *Time*—Morning.

Aroh—S R G P D S.

Avaroh—S D P, G R S.

Pakad—S D P G, D P G R R S.

6. *Basant Mukhari* is a Mishr Mel (mixture) of Bhairaon and Bhairava and known only perhaps to a very few experts. In its Purva Ang (1st half) it is Bhairava and in its Uttar Ang (2nd half), it is Bhairavi. It is quite obscure. It is so beautiful that it should be more popularised.

Jati—Sampoorna, *Vadi*—Dha, *Samvadi*—Re, *Time*—Morning.

Aroh—S R G M P D N S.

Avaroh—S N D P M G R S.

Pakad—S G M P D P D N S.

7. *Motaki* is the Raga of mixed category. Both Re and Nee are used. It is a Raga of Bhairavi Thata.

Movement of Notes :—S, D N S P, S, S M, P, G, R, S G, G, M R S.

8. *Uttar Gunakli* is also of Bhairavi Thata and being of mixed category it reflects the tinge of Asavari and Bhairavi.

Movement of Notes:—M G M P, D, P D M, M D M P G, G M R S, S R N, G R G M.

9. *Dhanashri* are of three kinds. One is under this Thata, the 2nd under Kafee Thata and the third under the Purvi Thata called Purya Dhanashri. These subtle differences are known to experts Re, Dha are dropped in Avaroh. It starts with Nee of Mandra.

Jati—Odava Sampoorna, *Vadi*—Pa, *Samvadi*—Sa, *Time*—Morning.

Aroh—N S, G, M P N S.

Avaroh—S, N, D, P, M, G, R, S.

Pakad—N S G M P N S, D P P G M P M G R S.

10. *Asawari* is obscure, Re Komal is classical, G N are dropped in Aroh.

Jati—Odava Sampoorna, *Vadi*—Dha, *Samvadi*—Re, *Time*—Noon.

Aroh—S R M P, D S.

Avaroh—S N D R, M G R S.

Pakad—M P S N D, P, M P G R S.

11. *Rag Mudrakee* is the Raga of Bhairavi Thata Both Ga, Ma, Dha and Nee are used in it.

Jati—Mixed Sampoorna, *Vadi*—Ma, *Samvadi*—Sa, *Time*—Night.

Aroh—S R G, M D, N S.

Avaroh—S N D, P D M G, R S.

Pakad—G M M P, M, G R S.

12. *Sarvari* is the Raga of Bhairavi Thata Both Re, Ga, Ma, Dha and Nee are used in it˙

Jati—Mixed Sampoorna, *Vadi*—Ga, *Samvadi*—Nee *Time*—All Times.

Aroh—S R G, M, P D N S.

Avaroh—S N D P M G R S.

Pakad—M P D P, M, G R S.

6

Bhairava Thata

Sa *Re* Ga Ma Pa *Dha* Nee Sa.

Bhairava Raga is one of the great God tunes. The shastric name of this Raga is Gound Malav Mel. The Ragas placed under this Thata are 21 out of which 6 are more popular :—

Bhairava, Kalingra, Ramkali, Bengal Bhairava Anand Bhairava Surashth, Aheer Bhairava Shiv mut Bhairava, Prabhat Bhairava, Lalit, pancham, Megh Ranjani, Gunkali, Jogia, Bibhas, Zeelaf, Gauri, Jangula, Dev Ranggani, Hajaz, Saverl, Des Goud.

1. *Bhairava*	4. *Gun kali*
2. *Kalingada*	5. *Jogiya*
3. *Romkali*	6. *Vibhas.*

Re Dha Komal are important in pointing to the fact that significance of Bhairava, Thata Ragas are Sandhi Prakash and melodies placed under this Thata are chiefly uttarang. Stress is laid upon Pa Dha Nee Sa. In all these malodies there is a great spirit of devotion, renunciation Devine praises and prayers. The themes are highly devotional, mystic, philosophic and soul stirring.

1. *Bhairava*, is one of the 6 great God tunes. It is the Thata Raga to be rendered only in the most difficult styles. It is an impressive, classical, popular melody, suitable only for men's voices, *Re Dha* (komal), is supreme and should be displayed in Andolan (swing), Dha is Vadi.

Jati—Sampoorna, *Vadi*—Dha, *Samvadi*—Ra, *Time*—Morning

Aroh—S R G M, P D, N Ṡ

Avaroh—Ṡ N D, P M G, R S.

Pakad—S, G M, P D P.

---

2. *Kalingra*, is extremely, popular. It lends itself to stirring religious appeal. Although the scale is Thata of Bhairava, but making Ma, prominent and Re, Dha not tremulous, the Rag changes its aspect and becomes quite distinct. Both Ma, are inserted in a captivating blend.

Jati—Sampoorna, *Vadi*—Dha, *Samvadi*—Ga, *Time*—Early Morning

Aroh—S R G M, P D N Ṡ

Avaroh—Ṡ N D P, M G R S

Pakad—D P, G M G, N, S R G, M.

---

3. *Ram Kali*, is slightly more known than Gun Kali, and is suitable for female voices, Ma, Nee, are wakra in the Aroh. It sounds well in medium and upper Octaves. Ram kali, is a dawn melody, and Ramkriya, (shastric), is a twilight melody. Both are Sandhi Prakash. Its special Tan, is Dha, Pa, Ma, Pa, Dha Nee, Dha Pa Ga Ma Re Sa Ma tivra and *Nee* komal, are inserted lending a charm.

Jati—Sampoorna, *Vadi*—Dha, *Samvadi*—Re, *Time*—Morning.

Aroh—S G, M P, D N Ṡ

Avaroh—Ṡ N D, P M P D N D, P G, M R S.

Pakad—D P, M P, D N D P G, R S.

---

4. *Bengal Bhairava* is obscure and is a heavy beautiful classical melody fit for Men's voices Nee, is dropped both ways. The combination of Sa, Dha, is significant Dha is Vadi.

Jati—Shadava, *Vadi*—Dha, *Samvadi*—Re, *Time*—Morning.

Aroh—S R G, M P D N Ṡ.

Avaroh—Ṡ D P, M G M R, R S.

Pakad—Ṡ D, P, GMP, R, R S.

---

5. *Anand Bhairava*, is also a Mishr Mel, and is a combination of Bhairava, and Bilawal. It is a heavy, and obscure, fit for men's voices. The Purva Ang is the Thata of Bhairava and Uttar Ang, is Thata of Bilawal.

Jati—Sampoorna, *Vadi*—Ma, *Samvadi*—Sa, *Time*—Morning.

Aroh—S R G M, P D N S.

Avaroh—S N D P, M G R S.

Pakad—P Ṡ D, P G M P, G M R S.

6. *Sourashth*, is a combination of Kalingra, Bengal and Pancham. It is quite obscure, Ma, is Vadi, Pa, is dropped in Aroh, and Nee, is weak. Both Dha, are used, tivra, in Aroh and komal in Avaroh. It looks like Bibhas, in its Uttar Ang, (2nd part), because of the Ma Dha, combination. It is a rare melody.

Jati—Shadava Sampoorna, *Vadi*—Ma, *Samvadi*—Sa, *Time*—Morning.

Aroh—S R G, M D, N Ṡ.

Avaroh—Ṡ N D, P M, G R S.

Pakad—Ṡ D, N Ṡ M D N Ṡ, R Ṡ, D, M R S.

7. *Aheer Bhairava*, is also a Mishr Mel, and is a combination of Bhairava and Kafee All these Bhairava, varities are rich and deep and can only be rendered by very clever professionals, Dha, natural is used in Aroh.

Jati—Sampoorna, *Vadi*—Ma, *Samvadi*—Sa, *Time*—Morning.

Aroh—S R, G M P, D N Ṡ.

Avaroh—Ṡ P, D P, M G, R S.

Pakad—S R R S, M R, M P D N Ṡ, P D, M R, G M P, M R, S R S.

8. *Shiv Mat Bhairava*, is a Mishr Mel, (combinatian of 2 Thatas) Todi, and Bhairava, which are most cleverly blended. The Aroh is Thata of Bhairava, and the Avaroh, is Thata of Todi, with Ga, Nee (komal). Such obscure intricate Ragas, can only be rendered by experts.

Jati—Sampoorna, *Vadi*—Dha, *Samvadi*—Re, *Time*—Morning.

Aroh—S R, G M P, D N Ṡ.

Avaroh—Ṡ N D P, N D P, M G M R S.

Pakad—D D P M P D N S N D P M G M R S G R S.

9. *Prabhat or Prabhati Bhairava,* is a Bhakti Marg, a highly devotional melody full of earnest and pathetic pathos. It should be sung in Bilampat, Rhythm and full of feeling. Both Ma, are used Vadi is Ma Prabhat is only known to expert. If it is sung in Drut Lay it would look like Kalingra, care should, therefore, be taken to bring out its particular characteristic.

Jati—Sampoorna, *Vadi*—Ma, *Samvadi*—Sa, *Time*—Morning.

Aroh—S R G M P, D N S.

Avaroh—S N D, P M, G R S.

Pakad—G M M D P N S.

10. *Lalit Pancham,* should be rendered in Mandra, and Madhya (Saptakas), is obscure known only to the experts. Pa, is dropped in Aroh, and only touched lightly in the Avaroh. Both Ma are used but shudh Ma, should be given prominence, Re Nee Dha Ma Ma, combination is peculiar of Lalit, and of no other Raga. It is one of the most beautiful melodies. *Vadi,* is Ma.

Jati—Shadav Sampoorna, *Vadi*—Ma, *Samvadi*—Sa, *Time*—Morning.

Aroh—S R G M, D N S.

Avaroh—S N, D P M, R G, M G, R S.

Pakad—S R N D N D P M P, M M G, M G R S.

11. *Megh Ranjini,* is obscure. Its Vadi, is Ma and sometimes both Ma, are touched. Pa, Dha, both was are dropped. The Nee, Ma, combination is peculiar. It looks like lalit also.

Jati—Odava *Vadi*—Ma, *Samvadi*—Sa, *Time*—morning.

Aroh—S R, G M, N S.

Avaroh—S N M, G R S.

Pakad—N R G M R, M M, N S N M, G R S.

12. *Gunkali* is to be sung in Madhya and Mandra Sthan, (middling and lower octaves). These rare Ragas are hardly ever heard in public. Ga, Nee, are dropped both ways. The Re, Ma, combination gives it a touch of Jogiya. Gun kali, is suitable for female voices

Jati—Odava, *Vadi Dha—Samvadi—Re, Time*—morning.

Aroh—S R, M P, D Ś

Avaroh—Ṡ D, P, M, G, R S.

Pakad—S R S, M P D, D Ṡ R M P, D Ṡ.

13. *Jogiya*, is another extremely favourite hymn. Such' songs are generally sung on Ektara, and the themes treat of rennuiciation and salf abnigation. Ga is dropped both ways. Dha, Ma, Ma, Re, is peculiar. It is a combination of Bhalrava and Asawari.

Jati—Odava shadava, *Vadi*—Ma *Samvadi*—Sa, *Time*—morning.

Aroh—S R M P, D Ś.

Avaroh—Ś N D P, D, M, R S.

Pakad—R M P, D M R S.

14. *Bibhas* is a rich heavy classical molody full of miraculous powers, known to great experts. It drops Ma, Nee, both ways, the Ga, Pa, combination becomes exceedisingly harmouious. The climax of the tune is Dha Pa. This is the only morning melody which drops Ma Nee Dha is vadi and is quite distinct. The counter part of Bibhas, is Rewa, which takes Ga, as vadi, is an evening melody of the same scale. There are fine ancient compositions in this wonderful Raga. It should be sung with dwelling upon notes at length for full effect.

Jati—Odava, *Vadi Dha, Samvadi*--Ga *Time*—morning.

Aroh—S R G, P, Ḋ S.

Avaroh—Ṡ D P G, R S.

Pakad—D D P, G P D P, G R S.

15. *Zeelaf* is Mishr Mel (mixture) Kalngra, Jaonpoori, Khut and Bharavi. It is rendered in the Kawali style, and with a tremor in the voice. Invented by Amir Khusro.

Jati—Odava, *Vadi*—*Dha, Samvadi*—Ga, *Time*—Noon.

Aroh--S G, M P D, Ṡ.

Avaroh—S D P, D M P, G M S.

Pakad—G M S, G G P D D M P, G M G.

16. *Gouri* is Sandhi prakash Raga. There is a decided touch of Kaliagra, and Shri in Gouri, Re, is Vadi, and Nee indicates the melody. A slight touch of Ma, tivra, is pleasing and appropriate. It is a religious rare beautiful melody only known to great experts.

Jati—Obava Sampoorna *Vadi—Re, Samvadi*—Pa, *Time*—Sunset.

Aroh—S R M P N S.

Avaroh—S N D P, M G R S.

Pakad—N S, R G R, M R, G R, P M P M, G R S.

17. *Jangula* is invented by Amir Khusro, now called Jangula. The style of Gut Toda played on the sister, is popular. As a song it is only known Kawali singers.

Jati—Odava Sampoorna, *Vadi*—Ma, *Samvadi*—Sa, *Time*—Morning.

Aroh—S R M P D S.

Avaroh—S D, P M, G R S.

Pakad—S R, M M P, D S, D P M P, G R S.

18. *Dev Ranjini* is a Raga of Southern System but is sung in North India also. Its category is Odava and Thata Bhairava. Re and Ga both are prohibited. Its vadi is Sa. It is more clear in Uttar Ang. N is some times used in its ascent,

Jati—Odava, *Vadi*—Sa, *Samvadi*—Ma, *Time*—Morning.
Aroh—S M P, D N S.

Avaroh—S N D, P M S.

Pakad—M P D S, M P M S.

19. *Hejaz* is based upon an old Arabic mode and invented [by Amir Khusrao. Like Zeelaf, it should be rendered with a piculiar shake and trill on the combination, Ga Dha, Dha Pa, Dha Nee, Ma, Pa, known only to some muslem experts of kawali style of singing-hejaz, is a mixture of Bhairavi and Bhairava.

Jati—Sampoorna, *Vadi*—Ma, *Samvadi*—Sa, *Time*—Noon.

Jati—S R G M P, N D S.

Avaroh—S N D P, M, G M P, N S.

Pakad—S N D P, M G M P, R S.

20. *Saveri* is obscure and southern melody. The Aroh, is the same as that of Jogiya, and Gunakali but the Avaroh is sampoorn, and this makes distinct. Ga Nee are dropped in Aroh. Vadi is Pa.

Jati—Odava Sampoorna, *Vadi*—Pa, *Samvadi*—Sa, *Time*—Morning.

Aroh—S R M P, D S.

Avaroh—S N D P M G R S.

Pakad—M P D P M P M G R S, R R S D S.

21. *Des Gaund* is the only Raga of Bhairava Thata which drops Ga Ma both ways and is therefore, quite distinct. It is rare and beautiful.

Jati—Odava, *Vadi*—Dha, *Samvadi*—Re, *Time*—Morning.

Aroh—S R S, P D N S.

Avaroh—S N D P, G R, S.

Pakad—D N S R N D P R P, R R S.

7

Kaliyan Thata

Sa Re Ga Ma Pa Dha Nee Sa

Kaliyan Thata is a counter part of the Bilawal Thata and takes Ma Tivra, hence, the Ragas placed under Kaliyan Thata are chiefly evening melodies. 16 Raga are placed under this Thata and out of which 10 are more popular.

Yaman—Yaman Kaliyan—Bhoopoli—Hamir—Kedar—Shudh Kaliyan—Kamode—Chhaya Nat—Gaud Sarang Hindole—Chander Kant—Sarani Kaliyan—Jet Kaliyan Shyam Kaliyan—Malsira—Pulindika.

1. *Yaman*	6. *Shudh Kaliyan*
2. *Yaman Kaliyan*	7. *Kamode*
3. *Bhoopali*	8. *Chhaya Nut*
4. *Hamir*	9. *Gaud Sarang*
5. *Kedar*	10. *Hindole*

The nature of this Raga resembles more with Bilawal Raga with the difference that this Thata is sung in evening prayers while Bilawal in morning prayers.

1. *Yaman* is the Kaliyan Thata Raga of Persian origin and is more or less obscure. Vadi—is Ga the Tan (Variation) Ma, Re, Ga, Re, Sa, is characteristic of Yaman only, and of no other Raga. Being Sampooran it lends itself to Alap (expansion) easily. It is sung in difficult styles. Yaman is distinct from Yaman Kaliyan, and this secret is known to the experts. It is suited for male voices.

Jati—Sampoorna, *Vadi*—Ga, *Samvadi*—Nee, *Time*—Evening.

Aroh—S R G, M P, D, N Ṡ.

Avaroh—S N D, P, M G, R S.

Pakad—N R G R, S, P M G, R, S.

2. *Yaman Kaliyan* is an extremely popular bright and charming melody, sung all over India, in all styles. Being Sampooran, it lends itself to Tans, and different laya (rhythm) suited for male and famale voices. It takes both Ma, and is a combination of Bilawal, Yaman and Kaliyan.

Jati—Sampooran, *Vadi*—Ga, *Samvadi*—Nee. *Time*—Evening.

Aroh—S R G, M, P D N, Ṡ.

Avaroh—Ṡ N D P, M, G M, G R, S.

Pakad—Ṡ N D P, M P, N D P, M G, M G R S.

3. *Bhoopali or Bhoop Kaliyan* is named ofter (Bhopal). A very popular dashing melody, suited to festive occasions and male and female voices. Bhoopali drops Ma, and Nee, both ways. At the time of singing protects it from Shudh Kaliyan, Jet Kaliyan and Deskar Ragas. Its vadi, is Ga, and therefore it is a Purva Ang, The combination of Ga, Pa, is always pleasant in the Raga in which Ma, and Nee, are obscure.

Jati—Odava, *Vadi*—Ga, *Samvadi*—Pa, *Time*—Evening.

Aroh—S R G P, D, S.

Avaroh—Ṡ, D P, G, R S.

Pakad—G R S, D, S R G, P G, D P G, R S.

4. *Hameer* is wakra Sampooran (not successive). Vadi swara is Pa, and in Aroh Ga is weak viz. Sa Nee Dha Pa Ga Ma Re, Ga Ma Nee Dha Pa Re, Pa Ga Ma Re Sa Ga Ma Dha. If the scale is taken successively it will become either 'Bilawal or Yaman'. Both Ma are used. The combination Ga, Ma, Dha, is exclusive to Hameer. It is a popular melody, to be sung in middling notes in Bilampat, is easy styles, fit for instruments of music and Lahria (special strain for dancing).

Jati—Wakra Sampooran, *Vadi*—Pa, *Samvadi*—Sa, *Time*—Night.

Aroh—ŚRS, GMD, ND, S.

Avaroh—S N D P, M P D P, G M R S.

Pakad—S, RS, GMD.

5. *Kedara* takes both Ma, its Vadi swara is Ma natural which is used frequently. In the Aroh Re, and Ga, are dropped and in the Avaroh Dha, Nee are dropped. The swara Ga is most insignificant in Kedara, Re, should never be used in Aroh. It is a very popular and bright melody suitable for all lighter styles, and also fit for intrumental music.

Jati—Odava Sampoorna, *Vadi*—Ma, *Samvadi*, Sa, *Time*—Evening.

Aroh—S͡M, M P, N D S.

Avaroh—S, N D, P, M P D P, M G R M S.

Pakad—S, M, MP, DPM, PM, RS.

6. *Shudh Kaliyan*, is obscure. Ma, and Nee, are dropped in the Aroh and in the Avaroh Nee, and Ma, are taken in Meno (Glide). If the Meno is not distinctly pronounced, it would loose its characteristic and would be more like Yaman Kaliyan. Vadi is Ga, or Re, Difficult styles may be performed in this melody. It is more suited to men's voices, and should [be sung in Bilampat (show rhythm) and in the middling notes. If Ga is retainened as vadi then it should be sung after Yaman.

Jati—Odava Sampooran, *Vadi*—Ga or Re, *Samvadi*—Dha or Pa, *Time*—Evening.

Aroh—S R G, P D S.

Avaroh—S N D P, M G, R S.

Pakad—G, R S, N D P S, G R, P R, S.

7. *Kamode*, Both Ma, are used, Vadi swara is Pa. The combination Re, Pa, distinguishes the Raga at once Ga, is wakra (crooked) in Avaroh viz. Sa, Nee, Dha Pa, Ga Ma Re Sa, and in Aroh Ga, and Nee, are dropped. A very popular pretty melody suitable for all styles, and instruments also for male and female voices.

Jati—Odava Sampooran, *Vadi*—Pa, *Samvadi*—Re. *Time*—Evening.

Aroh—S R, P, ́M P, D P, N D S.

Avaroh—S, N D, P, M P D P, G M P G M R S.

Pakad—R, P M̄ P, D P, G M P, G M R S.

8. *Chhaya Nut* is wakra (croked) Sampooran both ways. Both Ma, are used. The Vadi swara is Re. The combination Pa, Re, is characteristic of this Raga, Dha is prominent to keep Chhaya Nut distinct from Kamode. The following rules should be remembered Ga, and Ma, are taken in Aroh, the chief combination is Pa, Re, and not Re, Pa, like Kamode

viz. Kamode Tan, is Sa, Re, Pa, Pa, Ga Ma, Dha Pa, Dha, Pa Ga Ma Pa Ga Ma Re Sa. Chhaya Nut Tan, is Dha Pa Re Re Ga Pa Ma Pa Ga Ma Re Sa, Kamode is Uttar Ang (2nd half). Chhaya Nut is a Purva Ang Raga (1st half) A popular pleasing melody, suitable for instrumental and vocal music and also for both sexes.

Jati—Wakra Sampoora, *Vadi*—Pa, *Samvadi*—Re, *Time*—Evening.

Aroh—S, R G, M P, N D S.

Avaroh—S N D P, M P D P, G M R S.

Pakad—P, R, G M P, M G, M R S.

9. *Gaud Sarang* is wakra Sampooran. Both Ma are used. Its Vadi is Ga. Its special feature is Nee Sa Ga Re Ma Ga Pa Re Sa. An extremely beautiful popular melody suitable for all styles and for all voices also for instrumental music.

Jati—Sampooran Sampooran, *Vadi*—Ga, *Samvadi*—Dha, *Time*—Day.

Aroh—Ś, G R M G, P M D P, N D Ś.

Avaroh—Ś D N P, D M P G, M R, P, R S.

Pakad—S, G R M G, P R S.

10. *Hindole* is one of the 6 great God tunes. It is an ancient heavy classical melody, representing Krishna singing, surrounded by Gopikas to be rendered in the difficult style, only vocally or instrumentaly also on the classical Veena, Saroda, and Rubbab Bakar, for male voices and popular with artists. In Hindole Re, and Pa, are dropped both ways. Vadi is Dha. In Aroh Nee, is dropped and in Avroh it is wakra, and Ga, Sa, should be taken in meend like that—Sa Ga Ma, Dha Sa, Nee Dha Ma Ga Sa.

Jati—Odava—*Vadi*—Dha, *Samvadi*—Ga, *Time*—Day.

Aroh—SG, M D N D, S.

Avaroh —S, N D, M G, S.

Pakad—S, G, M D N D M G, S.

11. *Chandra Kant* is obscure, Ma is dropped in Aroh. Vadi is Ga, and therefore it is a Purvang Rag. Chandra Kant resembles with Yaman Kaliyan and Shudh Kaliyan. In Yaman Kaliyan, Aroh and Avaroh are 'Sampooran' and have good scope for variations. In Chandra Kant the Aroh is Sampooran. In Shudh Kaliyan Ma and Nee are dropped in Aroh, and in Avaroh Ma and Nee are weak and will be rendered with a meend, and not pronounced as in the former. Both the latter songs should be sung in the middling notes in Bilampat laya.

Jati—Shadav *Sampooran*, *Vadi*—Ga, *Samvadi*—,Nee, *Time*—Night.

Aroh—S R, G P, D N S.

Avaroh—S, N D, P, M, G R S.

Pakad—S, G G, M G. N, M P G, R N, R G.

12. *Savani Kaliyan* is a comparativtly modern variety of Kaliyan, invented by Muslim experts and is obscure. Ma, is dropped both ways, Nee is weak in Avaroh, Sa, is Vadi. This Rag should be sung in the middling notes in Bilampat, and this distinguishes itself clearly from 'Yaman Kaliyan' and 'Bhoopali', Jet, Savani and Chandra Kant are only known to great experts.

Jati—Shadav, *Vadi*—Sa, *Samvadi*—Pa, *Time*—Evening.

Aroh—S N D P, S R S, G P D S.

Avaroh—S N D, N D, P G R S.

Pakad—S MD, P G, D P G.

13. *Jet Kaliyan* is more or less obscure and drops Ma, and Nee both ways. It is much like Bhoop, and its Vadi is Pa. The 2nd variety of Jet goes under the Marva Thata and takes Re, (Komal) suitable 'for' 'Dhrupad and Dhamar' styles of singing it is to be sung in the middling notes and in Bilampat laya.

Jati—Odava—*Vadi*—Pa, *Samvadi*—Sa, *Time*—Evening.

Aroh—S R G, P, D P, S.

Avaroh—S D P, G P G, R S.

Pakad—SG, P, G P, D G P, D P R S.

14. *Shyam Kaliyan* is obscure and takes both Ma. Its vadi Swara is Sa, and looks like Kamode, the Re, Ma, combination looks something like Gound Malhar but Nee, pronounced distinguishes it from Kamode and Gound Malhar. By touching Dha, in Avaroh and retaining the Re, Pa, combination gives it an exquisite touch. It is a graceful melody to be sung in difficult styles.

Jati—Shadav Sampooran, *Vadi*—Sa, *Samvadi*—Ma, *Time*—morning.

Aroh—N S, M R, M P, D P, N S, N S.

Avaroh—S N D P, M P D P, G M R S.

Pakad—N S R, M P, D P, R, N S.

15. *Malsari*, is more or less obscure, Re, and Dha, re dropped both ways and Pa is vadi, Experts call Malsari, a Ragni of 3 swaras only and they lay full force on Sa Ga, and

Pa and Ma, and Nee, are extremely weak. It is a very graceful pretty melody known to the experts only, fit to be sung with both voices, also instrumentally and vocally.

Jati—Odava, *Vadi*—Pa, *Samvadi*—Sa, *Time*—Afternoon.

Aroh—S G, M P, N Ṡ.

Avaroh—Ṡ, N P, M G, S.

Pakad—P, P, G S, Ṡ, N P, M G, P, G S.

16 *Raj Pulandika*, is the Rag of the Kaliyan Thata M is used in it.

Jati—Odava, *Vadi*—Re, *Samvadi*—Dha, *Time*—Evening.

Aroh—S R M D N S.

Avaroh—S N D M R S.

Pakad—M D N D S.

8

Marva Thata

Sa *Re* Ga Ma Pa Dha Nee Sa.

At the time of Raga Ragini system Marva Raga was Considered as the Ragini of Shri Raga. Now-a-days it is popularly known as That Vachak Raga. 15 Ragas are placed under this Thata out of which 6 are more popular.

Marva—Sohini—Puriya—Lalit—Purba—Puriya Kaliyan Maligaura—Jet—Baradi—Bibhas—Pancham—Bhatyar—Bhankhar—Sajgiri—Lalit gauri.

1. *Marva*
2. *Sohni*
3. *Puriya*
4. *Lalit*
5. *Vibhas*
6. *Baradi*

The nature of this Ragas is *Shant* and, hence the melodies are meinly do Menateng in *Veer* and *Shant Rasas*.

1. *Marva* is one of the heavy big Raga fit only for difficult styles and male voices. The theme of this melody is fit for the booming of the guns, proclamation, and such cremonial occassions. Each note has to be pronounced forcibly. Marva, is only known to experts. Vadi is Ga, and Pa, is dropped altgether both ways Re, Ga, Dha, are prominent. In Aroh Nee is wakra (crooked) and in Avaroh Re, should be rendered wakra, so as to bring out its characterstic. The delicate subtleties of voices like Meend. Each tone should be pronounced with force. Marva marks the approach of Kaliyan.

Jati—Shadav, *Vadi*—Re, *Samvadi* Dha, *Time*—Evening.

Aroh—S R, G M D, N D S.

Avaroh—S N D, M G R S.

Pakad—D M G R, G M G, R S.

2. *Sohini* is of modern invention. It is an appealing most stirring melody and lends itself to intense feeling of sorrow, resting on the tearful Re, Sa, brings forth tears. Sohini, is popular. Vadi is Dha, komal Ma is used occasionally. The upper Sa, is affective. As the higher notes become prominent, it suggests the rise of the sun, therefore, Sohini, indicates the backoning of day light. Similarly Purya, its counterpart marks, the approach of the shades of night. It is a highly artistic and scientific arrangement. The Ga, Dha, combination is popular. A slight introduction of Dha, komal, is sometimes endulged in, such introductions are always the privilege of the experts who do it with great knowledge and add to the beauty. Re Pa, are dropped in Aroh, and Pa, is dropped in Avaroh also. Only Pa is dropped both ways now a days.

Jati—Shadav, *Vadi*—Dha, *Samvadi*—Ga, *Time*—Night.

Aroh—S G M D N S.

Avaroh—S R S, N D G M D M G R S.

Pakad—S, N D, N D G, M D N S.

3. *Purya* is a heavy beautiful melody. Vadi is Ga, Marva and Purya, take the same scale, but the distinction is marked by the Pakad (catch). Care should be taken to render Purya in the Madhya and Mandra Sthan. (middle and lower Octaves). If the same was rendered in Tar (Upper Octave) it would become Sohini. Its special Tan is, Ga, Nee Sa Nee Dha Nee Ma Dha *Re* Sa Nee *Re* Ga Nee *Re* Sa. Its combinations Re Nee, is special and should be enforced. All these subtle differences if borne in mind keep the melody quite distinct Purya has 5 varieties. Each is different from the other. The experts have the accurate knowledge viz:

1. A mixture of Lalit and Poorbi   creates Hindole Purya.
2. „   „   „ Bhairava and Purya   „   Bhairava Purya.
3. „   „   „ Lalit and Bihagra   „   Bihag Purya.
4. „   „   „ Lalit and Yaman   „   Yaman Purya.
5. „   „   „ Hindole and Dhaneshri „   Purya Dhanahri.

Jati—Shadav, *Vadi*—Ga, *Samvadi*—Nee, *Time*—Evening.

Aroh—N R S, G M D, N R S.

Avaroh—S N D M G R S.

Pakad—G N R S, N D N, M D R S.

4. *Lalit* is one of the most beautiful highly classical melodies, and if it is sung of the right hour with correct intonation, it transports one into a higher realm altogether. All such melodies should be enjoyed in Bilampat, dwelling upon each note for full effect. Lalit drops Pa, altoghether. Vadi is Ma, its exquisite combination is Dha, Ma, Dha Ma Ma Ga, Nee *Re* Ga Ma Ma Ma Ga *Re* Sa Nee *Re* Nee Dha.

Jati—Shadav, *Vadi*—Ma, *Samvadi*—Sa, *Time*—Night.

Aroh—N R G M M M G M D S.

Avaroh—R N D M D M G M R S.

Pakad—N R G M, D M, D M M, G.

5. *Purba* is the Raga of mixed category formed with the combination of Purbi, Puriya and Marva. It owes its origin to Marva Thata. Pa is prohibited and both Dha are used in it. Its vadi is Ga.

Jati—Shadava, *Vadi*—Ga, *Samvadi*, Dha—*Time*—Evening.

Aroh—N R G, M G, M D N S.

Avaroh—S N D, M D M G, R S.

Pakad—G N. D M G R S.

6. *Purya Kaliyan,* is a mixture of Marva and Kaliyan. It is only once in a way that one may hear it. Purya Kaliyan, is a Mishr Male mixture. Such Ragas are the outcome of knowledge and originality on the part of the composer. Some melodies get into fashion and obtain prominence and popularity. Others glide away into oblivion. Any melody rendered with knowledge is beautiful and inspiring.

Jati—Sampooran, *Vadi*—Re *Samvadi*—Dha *Time*—Afternoon.

Aroh—S R G M P N D S.

Avaroh—S N D P M G R S.

Pakad—P M G M G R S N D P M R S.

7. *Maligoura,* is modern and quite obscure. It is a mixture of Purya, and Shri Rag, and should be sung in Mandra and Madhya Saplakas (Middle and lower Octaves), and in Bilampat

Rhythm. Re is Vadi, by dropping Dha, it becomes distinct to all others. Some maintain that both Dha, should be used, with Re as Vadi. The third way is to give prominence to Pa in Pooriya and it becomes Maligoura. All such graces depend upon the knowledge and genius of the performer.

Jati—Sampooran, *Vadi*—Re, *Samvadi* Pa *Time*—Evening.

Aroh—S R S, N D P, S R G M P D N D S.

Avaroh—S N D P M G R S.

Pakad—R S N D P M G M D N R S.

8. *Jet*, is known to some singers, Ma Nee, are dropped both ways. Vadi is Pa, Ma, Nee, are dropped in Reva and Bibhas also but the Vadi and Pakad mark the distinctive feature of each melody, thus the confusion is avoided. There are 2 Jets. One of the Marva Thata is Jet Shri. The other one is Jet Kaliyan, of the Kaliyan Thata.

Jati—Odava, *Vadi*—Pa, *Samvadi*—Sa, *Time*—Evening.

Aroh—S R G P D S.

Avaroh— S D P, G R S.

Pakad—S G P, D G P, G. R G, P D G R S.

9. *Berari*, is quite obscure Ga, is Vadi Ma is weak; so the combination of Ga Pa, becomes naturally prominent. Berari should be sung with Andolit (swing) which is its characterstic. Berari has 11 varieties viz. 1 Shudh 2. Kuntal, 3. Dreventri, 4. Sendher, 5. Apsara, 6. Mak Sura, 7. Pratap 8. Todi Berred 9. Nag 10. Shok Berari. and Kallan Berari.

Jati—Wakra Sampooran *Vaāi*—Ga, *Samvadi*—Dha, *Time*—evening.

Aroh—S R G M P M D S.

Avaroh—S N D P M G R S.

Pakad—P P D, G P M, D M, G M R G, P G, R S.

10. *Bibhas*, there are 3 varieties, one is in Bhairava Thata, and is extremely devotional, Dha, is Vadi. Its special combination is Ga Pa, Ma Dha, Bibhas is a Malhar Mel. Purva Ang is that of Gouri and Uttar Ang, is that of Deskar. The 3rd kind is in the Bilawal Thata. All the 3 varieties are equally adorable.

Jati—Sampooran *Vadi*—Dha *Samvadi*—Ga, *Time*—Morning.

Aroh—S R S, G P, D M P, D N S.

Avaroh—S N D, P M G, P G, R S.

Pakad—P G, M D, N D, D P, G R S.

11. *Pancham*, is something like Bhatyar, and should be sung after Paraj. Bhatyar Pancham and Bhankhar are of modern invention. They are classical extremely beautiful melodies. The morning Pancham is the counterpart of Marva. It has 3 varieties. Lalit Pancham, Basant Pancham, and Hindole Pancham. All have drifted into obscrurity Ma, is Vadi. Both Ma, are used, and it takes a tinge of Lalit. Experts sing Pancham in 2 or 3 ways by dropping Re, and Pa, but this sort of licence is always endulged in.

Jati—Sampooran, *Vadi*—Ma, *Samvadi*—Sa. *Time*—Night.

Aroh—S R G, G M, P M, D N S.

Avaroh—S N P M, D M G P, G R S.

Pakad—M D S, N D M, D M G, M G. R S.

12. *Bhatyar* is invented by Bharat Hari Raja and is a mixture of Lalit, Kalingra and Paraj; and should be more popularised. In Uttar Ang it is like Mand, You can sing Bhatyar on Khamaj Thata also. Both Ma are prominent. Ma is Vadi. The combinations of Dha, Ma, is freely used. Ga Pa is another pleasant combination.

Jati—Odava Sampooran, *Vadi*—Ma, *Samvadi*—Sa, *Time*—Night.

Aroh—S R S, G M D S.

Avaroh—S N D P, M G M, G R S.

Pakad—S D P M, P G M, D P M G R S.

13. *Bhankhar*, both these melodies Bhatyar and Bhankhar, are so fascinating that they should be more popularized. Both Ma are used. Pa is Vadi. It takes Ma and Nee, therefore it becomes different to 'Bibhas' of Marva Thata, Ma, is not as distinct and frequent, therefore it is distinct from Bhatyar.

Jati—Sampooran, *Vadi*—Pa, *Samvadi*—Sa, *Time*—Night.

Aroh—S R S, G M D S.

Avaroh—S N D P, M G M, G R S.

Pakad—M D S, N D P M, P M G R S.

14. *Sazgiri,* is of modern invention and is a mixture of Parya and Pooravi. It should be rendered in Madhya and Mandra Sthanas. Ga is Vadi, Both Dha, are used, and Nee, Ma, forms the combination. A tinge of Ma, shudh is also introduced.

Jati—Sampooran, *Vadi*—Ga, *Samvadi*—Nee, *Time*—Evening.

Aroh—N R G R, G M P D. N S.

Avaroh—S N D P, D M G R , D M G R S.

Pakad—S R G M, R M R G S.

15. *Lalit Gauri* is special Raga of Marva Thata. Some singers include it in Pooravi Thata but on account of the use of both Dha and both Ma, it is accepted as a Raga of Marva Thata. It is made up of the combination of Gauri and Lalit hence called Lalit Gauri. Its Vadi is Re.

Jati—Sampooran, *Vadi*—Re, *Samvadi*—Pa, *Time*—Evening.

Aroh—S, R G, M P, D N S.

Avaroh—S N D P, M P G R S.

Pakad—M D N R G R S.

9

Pooravi Thata

Sa Re Ga Ma Pa Dha Nee Sa.

The Shastric name of this Raga is Ram Kiriya. The difference between Bhairavi Thata and Pooravi Thata is that of Madhyam (Ma). i.e. Bhairavi takes Ma Shudh and Pooravi takes Ma Tivra. Tody Thata takes Ga Komal and Pooravi takes Ga Tivra, 16 Ragas are placed under this Thata, out of which four are more popular.

Purvi—Shiri—Pooriya Dhanashiri—Basant—Paraj—Gauri—Tirveni—Shritank—Malvi—Bibhas—Rewa—Jiteshari—Deepak—Hans Naraini—Manohar—Kumari.

1. *Pooravi*
2. *Shri*
3. *Pooriya Dhanashri*
4. *Basant*

1. *Pooravi*, is the Thata Raga and fit for male voices. It is a heavy classical melody and lends itself to difficult styles only. It sounds well in Shahnai (flute) on the banks of a sacred river. Both Ma, are used Komal Ma only in Aroh. Its Tan is Nee Sa Re, Ga Ma

Ga Ma Pa Dha Ma Pa, Ga Ma Ga.

Jati—Sampooran, *Vadi*—Ga, *Samvadi*—Nee, *Time*—Evening.

Aroh—S, R, G, M P, D, N S.

Avaroh—S N D P, M, G, R S.

Pakad—N S R G, M G, M G, R S.

2. *Shri Raga*, is one of the great God tunes to be rendered only in the very heavy and difficult styles and sung in Billampat (slow speed) for full effect suitable for Male voices. Re, is Vadi. It crops Ga Dha, in Aroh. The combination of Re Pa, is exclusive.

Jati—Odava Sampooran, *Vadi*—Re, *Samvadi*—Pa, *Time*—Evening.

Aroh—S R R, S R M P, N S.

Avaroh—S, N D, P M G R, G R R S,

Pakad—S R R, S P, M G R, G R R S.

3. *Pooriya Dhanashri*, is an extremely beautiful melody and should be more popular. It should be rendered in the difficult styles only. Care should be taken to keap it distinct from Shri and Bhimplasi. There are many kinds of Purya but this is only one existing the rest are extinct. Pooriya Dhanshri, is a blend of Pooriya and Dhanshri. Shudh Ma, is dropped. Its Tan is Ma, Re Ga Re Ga Re Nee Dha Pa Nee Re Ga Ma Pa Dha Pa Ma Ga Ma Re Ga Re Sa. It is Purya Ang and Pa is vadi.

Jati—Sampooran, *Vadi*—Pa, *Samvadi*—Re, *Time*—Evening.

Aroh—N R G M P, D P, N S.

Avaroh—R N D P, M G, M R G, R S.

Pakad—N R G, M P D P, M G, M R G, D M G R S.

4. *Basant,* is to be sung in the season of 'Basant'. It is an extremely fascinating lovely melody. The theme treats with the season, the dainty yellow daffodils swaving in rhythm. The exquisite colour of Basant is worn in those days.

Jati—Sampooran, *Vadi*—Sa, *Samvadi*—Pa, *Time*—Night.

Aroh—S, G M D R S.

Avaroh—R N D, P, M G, M G M D M G R S.

Pakad—M D, R S, R, N, D. P, M G, M G.

5. *Paraj,* is an emotional beautiful dawn melody and full of spiritual feelings. Both Ma, are used, the upper Sa, is rendered again and again and sounds pleasant. It is very like Basant. Sa, is Vadi. Its special Tan is: Sa Re, Sa Re, Nee Dha Nee Dha Pa Ga Ma Ga Ma Dha Nee Sa and Sa Nee Dha Pa Ma Pa Dha Pa Ga Ma Ga.

Jati—Sampooran, *Vadi*—Sa, *Samvadi*—Pa, *Time*—Night.

Aroh—N S G, M D N S.

Avaroh—S N D P, M P D P, G M G M G R S.

Pakad—S N D P, M P. D P, G. M. G.

6. *Gauri,* is of two kinds. One comes under Bhairava Thata. In this, the Shri Ang is prominent. It is beautiful heavy fascinating melody when darkness spreads on the world. Ga Dha, is dropped in Aroh, and Ga is dropped in Avaroh, Nee of the lower Octave sounds very effective Re is Vadi. There are 8 varieties of Gauri. All are extinct.

Jati—Odava Shadav, *Vadi*—Re, *Samvadi*—Pa, *Time*—Evening.

Aroh—S R M, P N S.

Avaroh—S N D P, M R S.

Pakad—S N R N D D M, R S.

7. *Triveni*, is a pretty but obscure melody. Ma, is dropped so Ga Pa, form the combination in Avaroh. It retains the Shri Ang.

Jati—Shadava, *Vadi*, Re, *Samvadi*—Pa, *Time*—Evening.

Aroh—S R G P, D M S.

Avaroh—S N D P G R S.

Pakad—N R S, G P G R S.

8, *Shri Tank*, Tankya, or Tankra, is compratively modern and like Malvi and Triveni known only to experts. Shri Ang is prominent, Vadi note distinguishes the three ragas.

Jati—Shadava Sampooran, *Vadi*—Pa, *Samvadi*—Sa, *Time*—Evening.

Aroh—S R G P, D N S.

Avaroh—S N D P, M G R S.

Pakad—S P P, M D N D P P, M G, P G, R S.

9. *Malvi*, is a beautiful melody which retains the Shri Ang. Though it is modern, it is extinct Nee is weak in Aroh, and—Dha is weak in Avaroh Re is Vādi. The Ga Pa combination is always pleasant in the evening melodies.

Jati—Shadava, *Vadi*—Re, *Samvadi*—Pa, *Time*—Evening.

Aroh—S R G M P, M D S.

Avaroh—S. N P M G R S.

Pakad—S P G R S, G M D R S.

10. *Bibhas*, This Raga is of Pooravi Thata and is considered as of Sampooran Category. Ma and Nee are Weak. It is an Uttarang Raga. Some musicians use Ma (Sharp) in Avaroh. Nee is seldom used in Avaroh. The two forms of Bibhas are also used in Marva and Bhairava Thata. Stopping at Pa shows the tinge of Kaliyan Thata.

Movement of Notes—S, G, P, D.

Jati—Sampooran, *Vadi*—Dha, *Samvadi*—Re, *Time*—Night.

11. *Reva,* is modern and obscure Ma are dropped both ways. The Ga Pa combination is strong. The Shri Ang is enforeed. It is an appealing stirring serious melody.

Jati—Odava, *Vadi*—Re, *Samvadi*—Pa, *Time*—Evening.

Aroh—S R G P, D Ṡ.

Avaroh—Ṡ D P, G R S.

Pakad—G R G, R S, D P Ṡ, D P G P, G R S.

12. *Jeteshri,* is extinct. It is a mixture of Deskar, Berari, and Dholsari. It is a serious melody to be rendered in difficult styles, Ga is vadi' It is the only evening melody in which Re Dha is dropped in Aroh. Avaroh, it has the Poorvi Ang (form).

Jati—Odava Sampoorn, *Vadi*—Ga, *Samvadi*—Nee, *Time*—Evening.

Aroh—S G M, P N Ṡ.

Avaroh—Ṡ N D P M G R S.

Pakad—S G M D P N Ṡ.

13. *Deepak,* is one of the extinct great God tunes having mystic power over the supernatural force and excites fire in nature. It is to be sung by men, and treated with fear. It has been the favourite subject with artists.

Jati—Shadava, *Vadi*—Sa, *Samvadi*—Pa, *Time*—Evening.

Aroh—S G M P, D N Ṡ.

Avaroh—Ṡ D P M G R S.

Pakad—N R S, G M, P M, D P M, G R S.

14. *Hans Narayan,* is extinct. It is ancient Shastric melody known only to experts. The scale drops Dha Nee in Aroh and *Dha* in Avaroh.

Jati—Odava Shadava, a, *Vadi*—Sa, *Samvadi*— Pa, *Time*—Evening.

Aroh—S R G, M P S˙.

Avaroh—S˙. N P, M G, R S.

Pakad—S. R˙ N P, M G R S.

15. *Manohar*, is of Pooravi origin and is used for light songs. Pa is obscure in Avaroh.

Jati—Shadava Sampooran, *Vadi*—Ga, *Samvadi*—Dha, *Time*—All times.

Aroh—S, G, R, M, D, N S.

Avaroh—S˙ N, D P, G M G R S.

Pakad—D M G R, G R S.

16. *Rag Kumari* is the Raga of Pooravi Thata, Dha is dropped. It is the raga of Shadava Category and resembles with Sri Raga.

Jati—Shadava, *Vadi*—Re, *Samvadi*—Pa, *Time*—Evening.

Aroh—S R G M, P. N S˙.

Avaroh— S˙ N P, M G R, S.

Pakad—M G R, G R R S.

10

Todi Thata

Sa Re Ga Ma Pa Dha Nee Sa.

The Shastric name of this Raga is Nut Barali Mel but owing to the popularty of Rag Todi it is called the Todi Thata. At the time of Raga Ragini System it was the Ragini of Mal Kauns Raga. 7 Ragas are placed under this Thata, out of which *Todi* and *Multani* are more popular.

Todi—Multani—Gujri—Bahaduri Todi, Lachari Todi—Lakshami Todi—Anjani Todi.

When Todi is played on Beena the wild deer ventures with in meek submission and adoration on thrilling music.

1. *Todi,* is the Thata Raga. Although it is an extremely defficult, intricates and mystic Ragni. It is popular among the experts and they begin the exercises with the Tan Paltas (variations) of Todi. Dha, is Vadi, Ma' tivra, generally occurs in the evening melodies, but in Todi Goud Sarang and Hindole, morning melodies, Ma' tivra, is used, The formation of these Ragas, is such that they sound correct. Todi is to be sung in advance. morning, and Goud Sarang and Hindole should follow. Todi attracts wild deer in nature. It has been the favourite subjects for artists of all ages, who have hinted it.

Jati—Sampooran, *Vadi*—Dha, *Samvadi*—Ga, *Time*—Day.

Aroh—S, R, G, M P, D, N S.

Avaroh—S N D P, M G, R S.

Pakad—D N S, R G, R S, M G, R G R S.

2. *Multani,* is a highly classical popular favourite to be played on the shahnai, (flute) It sounds particularly soothing on the bank of a river. It carries a message from the unknown Pa which is Vadi, Re Dha are dropped in the Aroh, signifying the approach of afternoon melodies. Re, Dha, (Komal) indicate morning melodies Sa, Ma, Pa, are prominent in the afternoon. This secret is known to experts. In Multani, Ga, is Komal, is prominent. By making Ga, tivra, you get thc Poorvi Thata, hence Muntani, should proceed poorvi so that the ears may get reconciled gently and harmoniously to the dropping of Re, Dha, It must be remembered that the Ma', Ga, combination is peculiar in Todi, and should be rendered with Andolit, (swing).

Jati—Odava sampooran, *Vadi*—Pa, *Samvadi*—Sa, *Time*—Evening.

Aroh—N S, G M P, N S.

Avaroh—S N D P, M G, R S.

Pakad—N S, M G, P G, R S.

3. *Gujari,* is an elegant melody, represented as floating on waters on a bed of lotus. It is like Todi, but Pa is dropped both ways, therefore, it becomes distinct. Gujri is a beautiful melody.

Jati—Shadava. *Vadi*—Dha. *Samvadi*—Re. *Time*—Evening.

Aroh—S R, G M, D N S.

Avaroh—S N D M, G R S.

Pakad—D M G; M, D M G, R G R S.

4. *Bahaduri Todi,* was invented by Naik Bakhshoo who was a great vocalist in the reign of Sultan Bahadur of Gujarat. He named, it after his King as Bahaduri Tudi'. It is obscur and known only to exclusive families. It is a heavy beautiful melody and to keep its characteristic it should be rendered only in the middle and lower Octaves, and in the solemn grandeur of Bilampat rhythm. It is a court melody like Durbari. Vadi, is Dha of lower scale. Pa, is dropped in the Avaroh, and Ma Re, is its peculiar combination,

Jati—Sampooron—Shadava, *Vadi*—Dha Samvadi—Ga, *Time*—Morning.

Aroh—S R R M, P D N S.

Avaroh—S N D, M G, R S.

Pakad— D P. D R S, N. S G M, R S.

About the other Jatis of Todi like *Lachari Todi*, Laxami Todi and *Angani Todi* V. N. Bhatkhande has expressed his views in Vol. VI of Kramik Pustak Malika as follows :—

5. *Lachari Todi*. In Lachari Todi Shudha Re, both Ga, Dha and Nee are used.

6. *Laxami Todi*. In Laxami Todi the musicans of Rampur use both Re, Ga, Dha and Nee.

7. *Anjani Todi* is used mainly in Dhrupad Gayan and is more popular in Punjabi Gharanas. They suppose it as a Raga of Sampooran Category and use both Dha and Nee, Komal Ga and rest of the shares Shuddha. Its Purv ang is mixture of Desh and Uttarang of Kafee and Asawari.

METHODS OF RECITING RAGA AND RAGNIS

Raga and Ragnis were developed by the Buddha musicologists during the first centrury A.D. That was accomplished after the evolution of the Universal Scale of music.

The Buddha musocologists and theoreticians studied in depth the nature of males and females at large and eventually based Ragas and Ragnis developed by them on the nature of those males and females. They went a step further. They took into account such persons also who could perform the roles of males as well as females equally satisfactorily and eminently in dramatic performances. They named such persons as eunches
The Ragas which such persons or eunches represented were given the name *Nipunsak Ragas*. In other words, the following three types of Ragas were developed:

(1)   Ragas which displayed the nature of males.

(2)   Ragas which displayed the nature of females (and were called Ragnis), and

(3)   The Ragas which displayed the nature of both males and females equally effectively.

If we look carefully at the 10 *Thaths* described earlier, we note that there are some Ragnis which have been denoted as Ragas. That is a wrong tradition. It is very essential for an expert musician to sing a Raga keeping in mind the nature, emotions and sentiments of males. Similarly, at the time of singing Ragnis, the musician must keep in mind, the nature of females, their wishes, aspirations, emotions and sentiments. Then and only then would the musician be able to display and touch upon the essential elements of a Rag and its Ragni.

Names of Ragas and Ragnis falling under each of the ten Thathas are given below:

1.   *BILAWAL THATH* - It is a *Nipunsak Raga*. It should be sung keeping in mind the nature of a male.

The following Ragas fall under this Thath:

1.	Shudh Bilawal (Male)	5.	Deshkar (Male)
2.	Alhiya Bilawal (Male)	6.	Pahari (Female)

3.	Bihag (Male)	7.	Durga (Male)
4.	Shankara (Male)	8.	Maund (Male)

2. KHAMAJ THATH - It is a Nipunsak Male Raga. It should be sung keeping in mind the nature of a male.

The following Ragas fall under this Thatha:

1.	Khamaj (Male)	2.	Des (Male)
3.	Tilak Kamod (Male)	4.	Jai Jai Wanti(Female)
5.	Tilang (Male)	6.	Jhanjhoti (Female)

3. KAFI THATH - It is a Raga of a female nature. It should be sung keeping in mind the nature of a female. The following Ragas fall under this Thath.

1.	Kafi (Female)	2.	Bageshwari (Female)
3.	Brindabani Sarang (Female)	4.	Bhim Plasi (female)
5.	Peelu (Male)	6.	Gaur Malhar (Male)
7.	Mian Ki Malhar(Male)	8.	Bahar (Male)
9.	Suidhura (Male)	10.	Barwa (Male)
11.	Dhinashri (Female)	12.	Shudha Sarang (Male)
13.	Pat Manjari (Female)	14.	Naiki Kanhra (Male)
15.	Dev Sakh (Male)	'6	Megh Malhar (Male)

4. ASAWARI THATH - It is a Thath of female nature. The following fall under this cateogry:

1.	Aswari (Female)	2.	Jaunpuri (Female)
3.	Darbari Kanhra (Male)	4.	Adana (Male)
5.	Gandhari (Female)	6.	Sindh Bhairvi(Female)

5. *BHAIRVI THATH* - It is a thath of female nature. The following Ragas fall under it:

1.	Bhairvai (Female)	2.	Malkauns (Male)
3.	Bilas Khani Todi (Female)	4.	Komal Bageshwari (Female)
5.	Bhopali Todi (Female)	6.	Basant Mukhari (Female)
7	Motakki (Female)	8.	Uttar Gunkali (Female)
9.	Dhanashri (Female)	1(	Asawari (Female)
11.	Mudraki (Female)	1.	Saveri (Female)

6. *BHAIRVA THATH* - It is a Thath of male nature. The following fall under this category:

1.	Bhairva (Male)	2.	Kalingra(Male)
3.	Ram Kali (Female)	4.	gunkali(Female)
5.	Jogia(Male)	6.	Vibhas(Male)

7. *KALYAN THATH* - It is of male nature. It is classified into:

1.	Yaman(Male)	2.	Yaman Kalyan(Male)
3.	Bhupali(Female)	4.	Hamir(Female)
5.	Kedar (Male)	6.	Shudh Kalyan(Male)
7.	Kamod(Male)	8.	Chhaya nat(Male)
9.	Gaur Sarang(Male)	10.	Handol(Male)

8. *MARVA THATH* - This Thath is of male nature. It is categorised as under:

1.	Marva(Nipunsak Male)	2.	Sohani(Female)
3.	Pooria(Male)	4.	Lait(Male)
5.	Vibhas(Male)	6.	Barari(Female)

9. *POORAVI THATH* - It is of female nature. The following fall under this Thath:

1.	Pooravi(Female)	2.	Shri (Male)
3.	Pooria Dhanashari (Female)	4.	Basant(Male)
5.	Paraj (Male)	6.	Gauri(Female)
7.	Tirveni(Female)	8.	Shri Tauk(Male)
9.	Malvi(Female)	10.	Bibhas(Male)
11	Reva(Male)	12	Jiteshari(Female)
13	Deepak(Male)	14	Hans Narayani(Female)
15.	Manohar(Male)	16	Kumari(Female)

10. *Todi Thath*- It is of female nature. The following Ragas fall under it:

1.	Todi (Female)	2.	Multani (Female)
3.	Gujari (Female)	4.	Bhaduri Todi (Female)
5.	Lachari Todi (Female)	6.	Lakhshmi Todi (Female)
7.	Anjaani Todi (Female)		

NOTE:- Beginners are advised to learn Bilawal thath to begin with. They may do preferably with the help of qualified tutors. Even if they want to learn from books wi the guidance of a tutor, they should start with Ragas of the Bihawal Thath.

After acquiring sufficient experience of singing ragas of the Bisawal Thath, they shou switch on the singing of ragas of Kalyan Thath which ragas are of Ma(tivre) type.

Classical songs are classified with Dharupad, Dhammar ,Khayal, Chhota and Bara-Tappa Thumri, Tarana etc. Beginners should learn Chhota khayal first. They should then lear singing of bhajan and geet. After mastering them, they should attempt to sing other type. of classified songs.